LEN TABNER
1970 – 1989

LEN TABNER

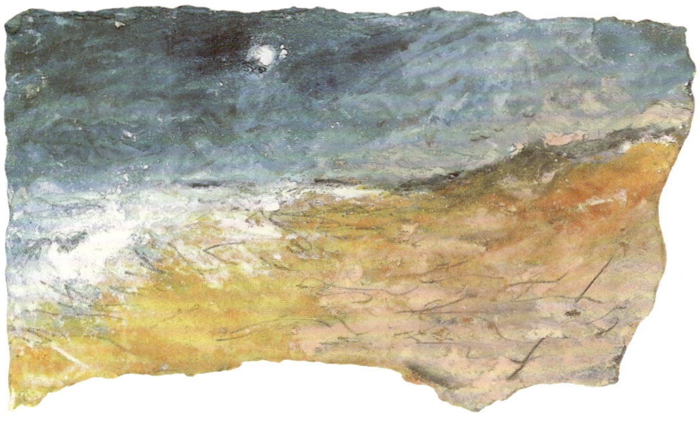

PAINTINGS & DRAWINGS
1970 – 1989

THOS. AGNEW & SONS LTD.
43 OLD BOND STREET, LONDON. WIX 4BA
TEL. 01 629-6176 FAX. 01 629-4359

Dedicated to the memory of my father and grandmother

Acknowledgements

The artist would like to thank all those people who have helped and co-operated on this project, particularly William Joll, and all at Thos. Agnew & Sons, Dr. David Brown, Peter Prendergast and Ian Macdonald.

Published by Thos. Agnew & Sons Ltd., 43 Old Bond Street, London, W.1.X. 4BA.
Telephone 01 629 6176. Fax. 01 629 4359.
I.S.B.N. 1 870434 03 X.

Photography. Prudence Cumming Associates, Dover Street, London.

Printed in Great Britain by Balding + Mansell plc

The small works in notebooks are intended to stand equally with those that are large. Neither is more nor less complete than the other. Both the small watercolour studies, and the large drawings are the result of direct confrontation with nature. An experience has demanded a response. The nature of the experience has dictated the form which the response has taken.

The cliff foot during severe storms in February, a series of studies of the sea. The pressure of wind and water upon boulders cast upon the shore, upon worn concrete sea walls and breakwaters, upon wooden piles, upon iron legs of Victorian piers, upon the limpet's shell.

Soft dampness of a dawn mist, lying over the saltings of a desolate estuary.

Dusk – a heavy shower, sitting neck deep in a dense wet clover field – wetter almost than the sea itself. Ribbon of velvet floating from eye to infinity.

Heat of summer – close to the house – sitting amongst hawthorn hedges, whilst wheat and barley silently ripen.

Again, frantic hours, as bales are stacked beneath lowering skies. The earth, itself, packaged: set out in the dying light. One contemplates the land with bewilderment as it changes hourly, and yet remains unchanged.

The earth moves, gently
        And stirs.
As earthworms turn.

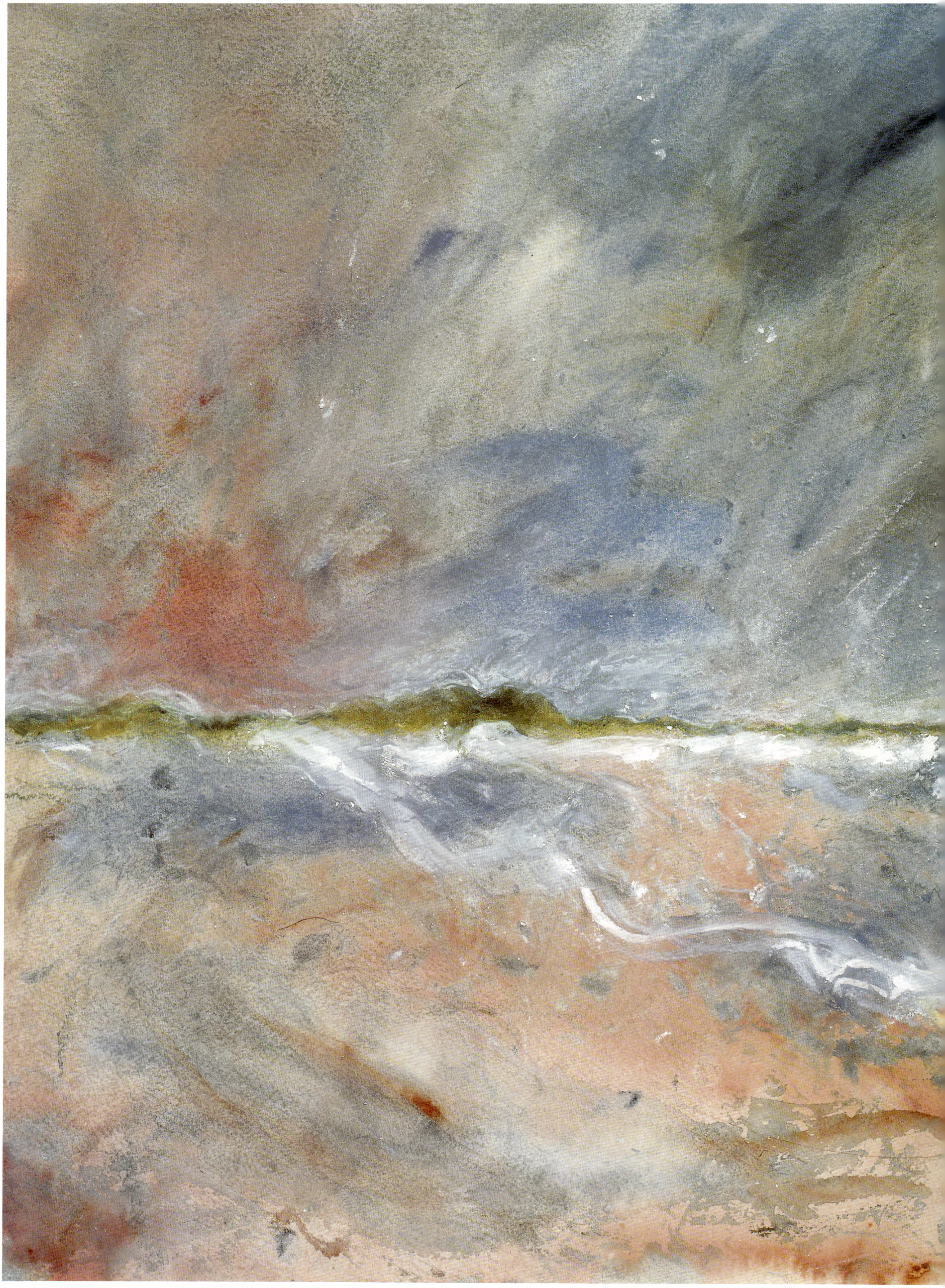

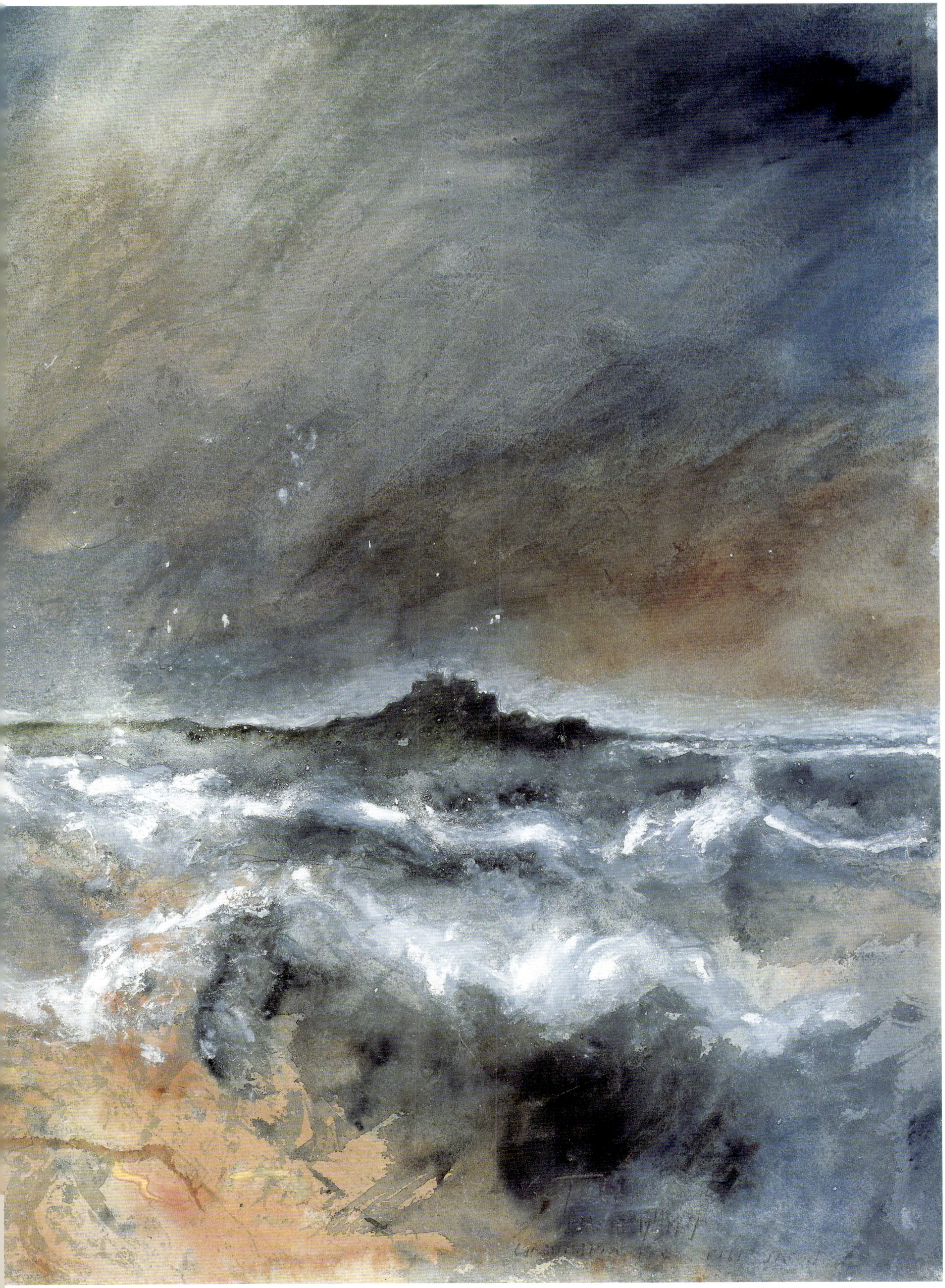

Lindisfarne from Ross Back Links. March 14th 1989. 23″×31″.

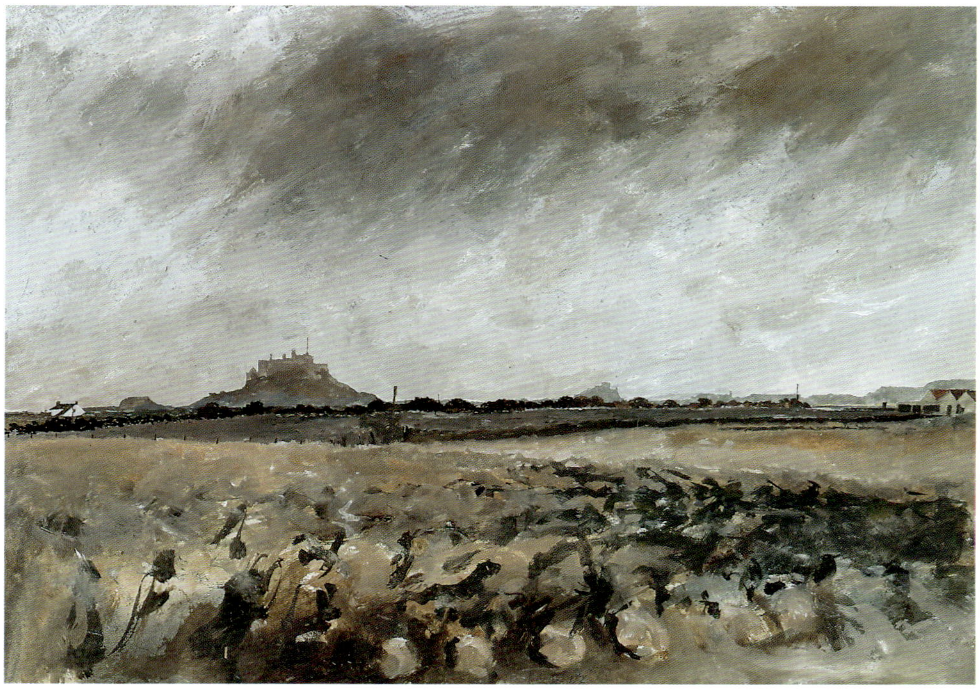

Turnip field, Lindisfarne Castle with Bamburgh beyond, dawn. March 1976. 13¼″×18½″.

Introduction

The sea has always been central to the life and work of the North Yorkshire painter Len Tabner. All his painting is done near, by, or on the sea. He was born in South Bank, then part of the old North Riding of Yorkshire, on the south bank of the River Tees; his father owned a Yorkshire coble (a fishing boat) of his own and worked for the Tees Conservancy Commissioners, who were charged with keeping the mouth of the Tees navigable. He ended up in charge of a dredger: from early childhood his son often accompanied him in a diverse variety of boats, fishing with long lines, nets and crabpots.

Len Tabner lives and works in East Cleveland, a few hundred yards from the highest cliffs in England, 650 feet above the sea: his pictures, rooted in the landscape of the North-East, reflect the changes that have taken place in thirty years. The development of the petro-chemical industries and the expansion of steel-making have changed the once open estuary of the Tees beyond recognition. Conscious of the adverse effects of pollution, but equally of the size and dramatic potential of the machinery and installations to be found in the area, Len Tabner adds an artist's awareness of the changing effects of light and weather to a landscape already rich in natural beauty.

I first came across Tabner's work while I was a buyer for the Contemporary Art Society: my liking for the work led me to meet the artist. I accompanied him on visits to places where he painted – the ironworks close to the Tees and the breakwater at Staithes – and on a painting trip to Lindisfarne in Northumberland. I even went with him down into the potash mine in Boulby, the deepest mine in Europe, and I have been able to observe how images of weather and water are laid onto paper with speed and skill. Some of the influences on his work are obvious: Turner and Constable for example, but Samuel Palmer and Paul Nash have also been important to Tabner. It seems to me logical to link his work with names like Piper, Sutherland, Bomberg, and that great original, William McTaggart (1835–1910), perhaps the greatest Scottish painter of the last hundred years. Because he has chosen to live and work in the North-East, he is too little known to a wider audience. I hope that a big showing of his work in London, coupled with the publication of this book will do something to rectify this imbalance.

David Brown, M.R.C.V.S.
September 1989.

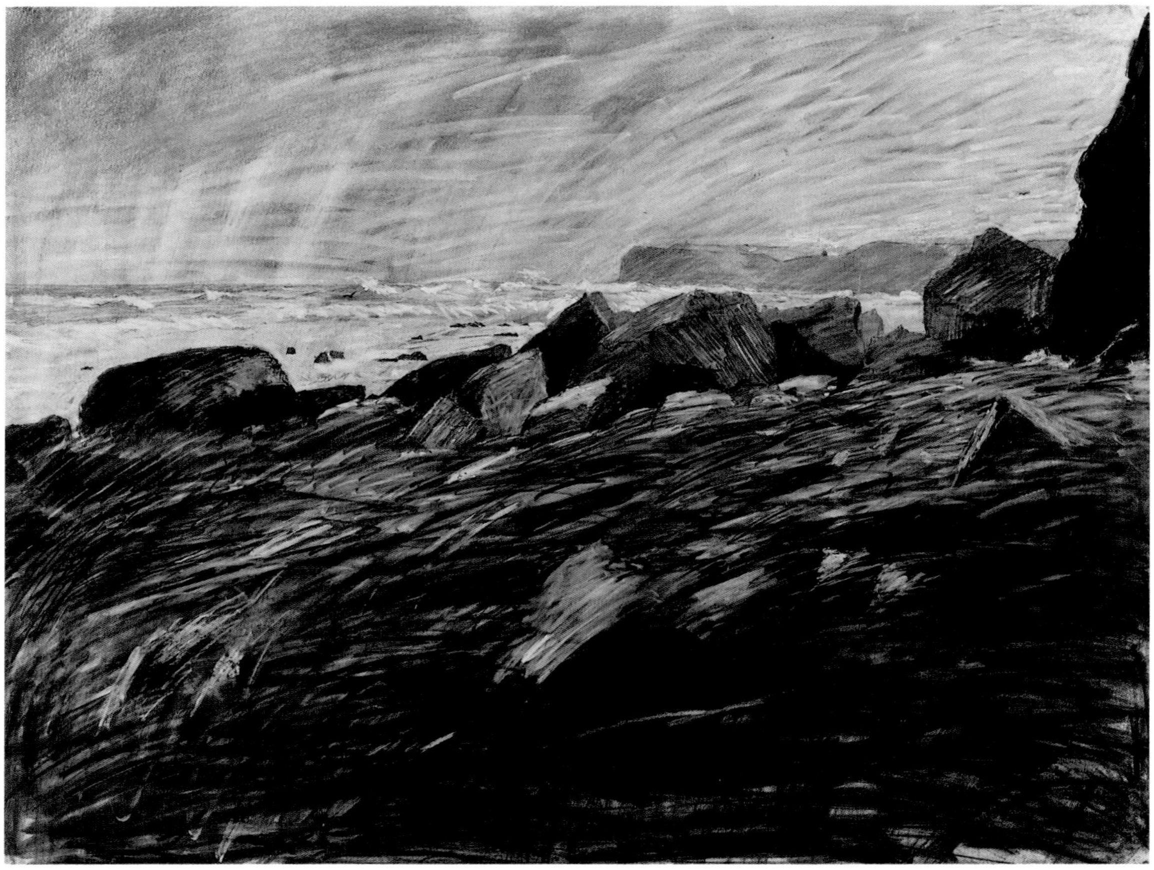

Boulders at the foot of Boulby cliffs. November 1972. Charcoal, pencil & Conté. 15″×20″.

THE ARTIST LEN TABNER

I first met Len Tabner 21 years ago when we were both post graduate students in painting at Reading University. I remember him arriving in his khaki army shorts. He'd cycled from Wiltshire where he had been a student at Corsham Court. His first concern was accommodation, but on discovering the coal cellar, he cleaned it out, painted it white and lived in it!

Reading University post graduate department was a place where we were allowed time to think and to establish our own identities as painters, each student was allowed to plan his own programme of work. Claude Rogers was Professor of Fine Art and Terry Frost one of the teachers and we were allowed visiting tutors of our own choice. I remember Howard Hodgkin, Martin Froy and Adrian Heath visiting Len. It was a very fertile time in the development of our work. Drawing at this time was unfashionable and the 10 students were of various degrees of commitment and talent. The studios were in an old Victorian house near the Royal Berkshire Hospital.

Len, an astute Yorkshire man, was wary of us all. He was born in South Bank on the River Tees, near Middlesbrough, and he had five sisters and one brother, all younger than himself. His father worked on small river craft and dredgers for many years and at that time was skipper on a workboat on the Tees. At an early age, to get a bit of peace and quiet Len moved to live with his Grandmother, a widow living a few doors away from his parents. Much of his time as a young lad was spent on the river banks, around the edge of the iron works and the ship yard, but especially on the river mouth at a place called the South Gare Breakwater, where his father kept a Yorkshire coble for inshore fishing and had a small wooden cabin. His father loved the sea and all things related to it, he had been a merchant seaman during the war and had a great influence on Len. They spent a great deal of time together fishing, working pots and longlines, working on the boat or stripping down and rebuilding boat engines or old motor bikes. Len's father had very little time for class or politics, believing that by hard work and thrift he could provide enough for his family to live on. He always managed to have his own boat and house and a vehicle to drive. The ability to survive is something that Len has inherited from his dad, and is one of the reasons why he is still painting, while fellow students have fallen by the wayside.

At the age of eleven, Len failed the entrance examination to the Grammar School and went to Victoria Street Boys Secondary Modern School at South Bank. It was here that he started painting and drawing. He actually spent most of his time in the art room although he was interested in many other subjects. At 13 he passed the entrance examination to the Grammar School. Here he met John Carter, an art teacher trained in Edinburgh who emphasised the need to study other subjects. While at the Grammar School he spent a great deal of his time bird watching, drawing, cycling and walking, with a fellow pupil Brian Smith. Apart from this he felt it to be the most uninspiring and wasteful time of his life.

With his knowledge of engines and his ability to make things, plus his gift for drawing, Len had the skills to be an engineer or an architect and this might well have been what his dad would have liked for him. However by the age of 10 he had made up his mind that he wanted to be an artist. For Len, being an artist has meant more than just painting and drawing; it has meant developing a way of living and surviving that encompasses everything that interests him.

On leaving school Len attended the art foundation course at Middlesbrough School of Art, an institution that had a long-standing tradition in the teaching of drawing. In 1965 Len went to study at Corsham Court in Wiltshire. The lushness of Wiltshire was completely in contrast to the steelworks and the coast around the Tees. The decision to go was a considered one, he had always wanted, even as a young boy, to go and live in a rural environment. The years at Corsham were the happiest and most fulfilling of his student life.

Corsham was very much a painting department of the 1960s. Adrian Heath, Martin Froy, Michael Kidner and Howard Hodgkin taught there, and it would be fair to say that the emphasis wasn't upon drawing. It was a very fertile period in which Len was able to pursue his other interests, particularly in nature, walking and adventure. It was at this time he designed several tents and made a rucksack based upon his study of polar exploration.

Whereas in Yorkshire his painting was developed from drawing, at Corsham he began to contemplate the possibility of non-figurative image making and became interested in the work of Klee and Kandinsky. It was there that Len met a fellow student called Ian Williams who introduced him to classical music and also to the works of such painters as Samuel Palmer, Stanley Spencer and Bonnard. During the years at Corsham they spent a great deal of time together walking and exploring the Wiltshire landscape. Eventually they both lived in the same farmhouse. It was also at Corsham that Len met the sculptor Helen de Paravicini who eventually became his wife.

The landscape of Wiltshire is very different to the industrial landscape of Teeside and when Len felt a need to be in a wilder place and nearer to the sea he travelled to Wales and to the coastline of Pembroke in particular. At other times he would go to Cornwall or further up to Yorkshire or Northumberland. His time was spent looking, walking and drawing. When he felt refreshed he would return to Wiltshire and try to channel his experiences into his painting.

Reading University was a contemplative time for Len. His paintings then were large and ambitious and non-figurative in concept. Nevertheless, much of the mark making, the long linear shapes and more broken up atmospheric sky like passages certainly came from his roots, the landscape of the North East, telegraph poles and winter skies, and all this was laying down the ground for his work after college.

The two years at Reading were a time for planning for the future. Although Len is very much a thinker and intuitive philosopher he also realised that he needed a vehicle for his energy and strength. In July 1970 he left Reading and headed for a cottage he had purchased in Boulby on the highest cliff in England. The cottage, though in a marvellous position above the 650 foot cliffs, hadn't been inhabited for many years. His needs were simple, to paint pictures, to make the house habitable and to provide the finance to do both.

He was fortunate in that during his final year at Corsham he had been commissioned by Sir Arnold Weinstock to design and decorate two rooms. One was a children's puppet theatre and another a train room with a massive layout which had to be decorated with a Swiss mountain landscape. This work had gone on much longer than intended and spilled over into the early years at Boulby providing enough money to work on the house and to start drawing and painting.

Once he had acquired sufficient funds from decorating work in Wiltshire he spent his time either building, or painting and drawing. He tried to work in a disciplined way but found that some days he wanted to draw so he allowed instinct to be the deciding factor.

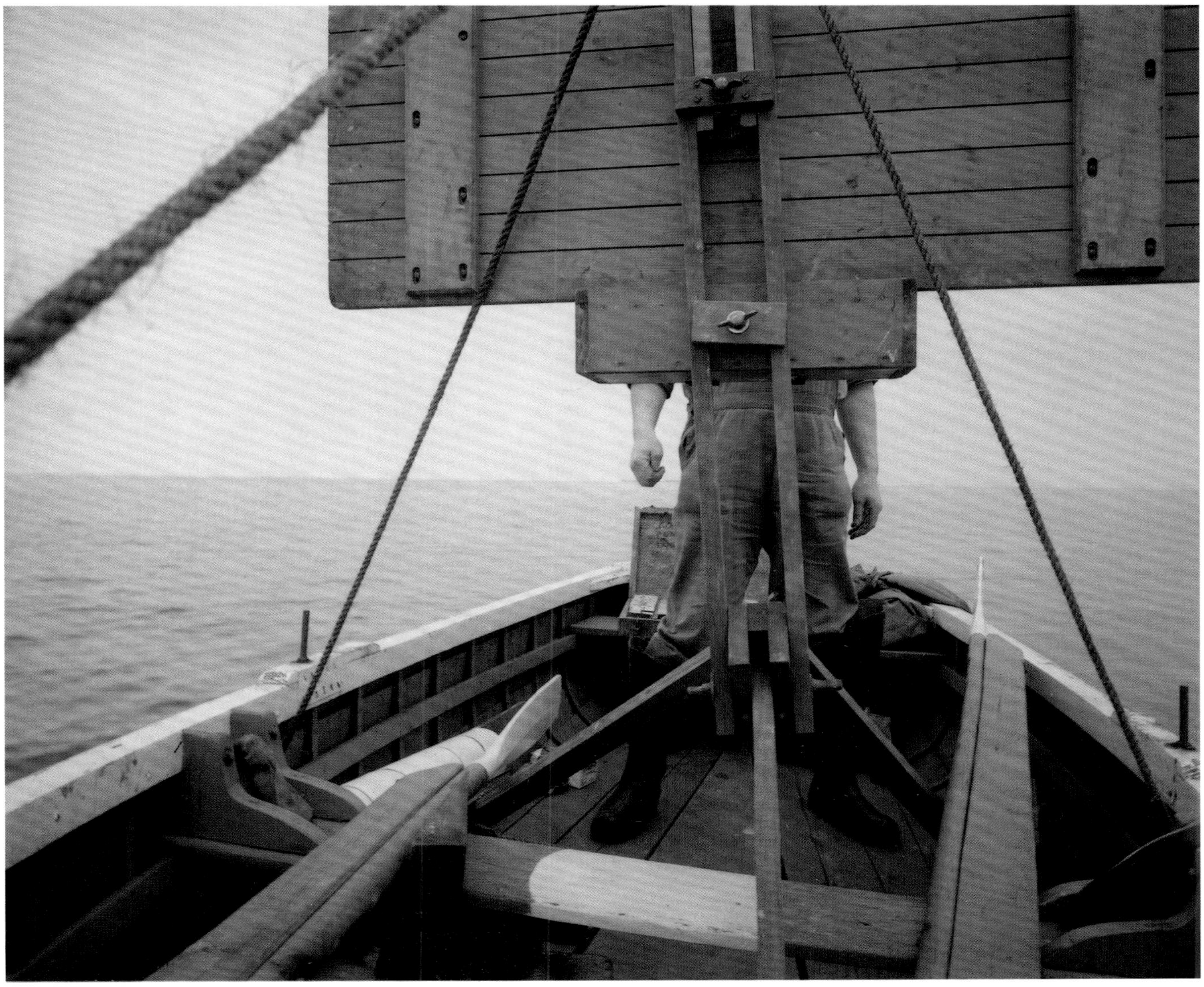

It would be wrong to write about Len, as a painter, without mentioning the development of the building of the house and his method of survival, all three are interrelated and important parts of his development. Don't imagine that the building work or the acquisition of materials was any ordinary activity. There was very little money and Len didn't want to use breeze blocks and ready-made windows and doors. The house had to have his stamp, a sense of personality and also to fit into the natural and traditional geographical environment of Boulby. The cottage was built out of blocks of sandstone, and in order to build extensions, Len heaved stone from various demolished buildings, including some from the bottom of Boulby Cliffs. To get timber for the roofs he searched the bank of the River Tees, and in the early 1970s he could be seen hauling them back on his motor bike and side car. There are beams in his house which are 20 feet long and 16 inches in the round that he put into place without machinery but by using tack and pulley. There are window frames of a traditional pattern that he built himself, there are small windows at various places, inserted so that the inhabitants can get a glimpse of the sea. In the corner of the garden is built a stone building, of such quality that the local planning officer couldn't understand why they hadn't discovered it before, and why it wasn't listed as a protected building.

Although Len has worked in oil paint, his main method of working has been water colour, chalk and pastel. For a period in the mid-1970s he also devoted some time to print making, lithography in particular. The subject matter has been landscape, the sea, the weather and industry. Much of Len's working drawings and studies are hardly exhibited as they are contained in specially made sketch books. Most of the work is done outside on the spot, at the sea's edge, at the bottom of the Potash mine, in Boulby or at the side of a lane where he has made many images of a particular hawthorn bush, drawing and painting it many times over the years.

The early work of the 1970s made around the fields of Boulby, of hay stacks, houses and the breakwater at Cowbar, are black and white and have a feeling of austerity. A rich kind of black and grey, it is as if in these early works he is disciplining himself to look and understand the place where he has chosen to live. In these early coast drawings he is trying to understand the rock formation and the infinite space of the sky, to understand the way the sea moves and the wind blows. In the drawings of Washington town, the brickworks and the old colliery, there is an awareness of a town disappearing, and the rush of red and rust when the buildings fall, the bricks splitting open. The drawings have a sense of urgency. They were made quickly, the buildings were often demolished overnight. The method of working was not that different to that of the war artist, needing to describe what was going on immediately, but at the same time trying to get a sense of poetry into the work.

The essential thing is to realise that working at Washington Town was a commission Len designed for himself and for which he then persuaded the authority to employ him. The condition was that they could have the work he produced if they supported him for three months. Of course the chances were that he would produce nothing, it was a gamble by the authority and a test of Len's professionalism. For weeks he did nothing, but after a while of observing and contemplating, the ideas and the work flowed. For a small amount of money, the authority acquired a set of visual records of the town, and Len was able to do a bit more on the house and then move onto the next set of paintings.

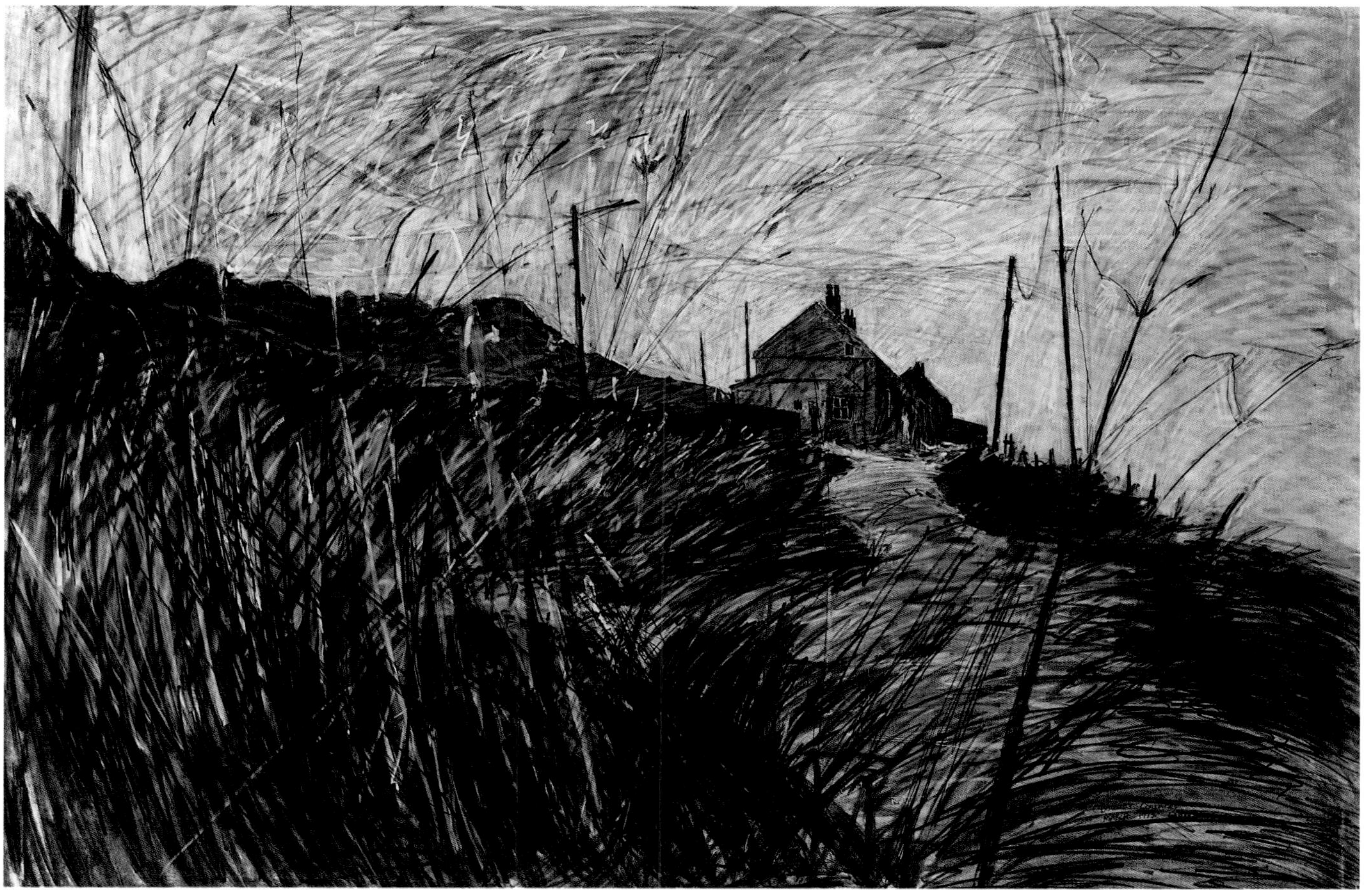

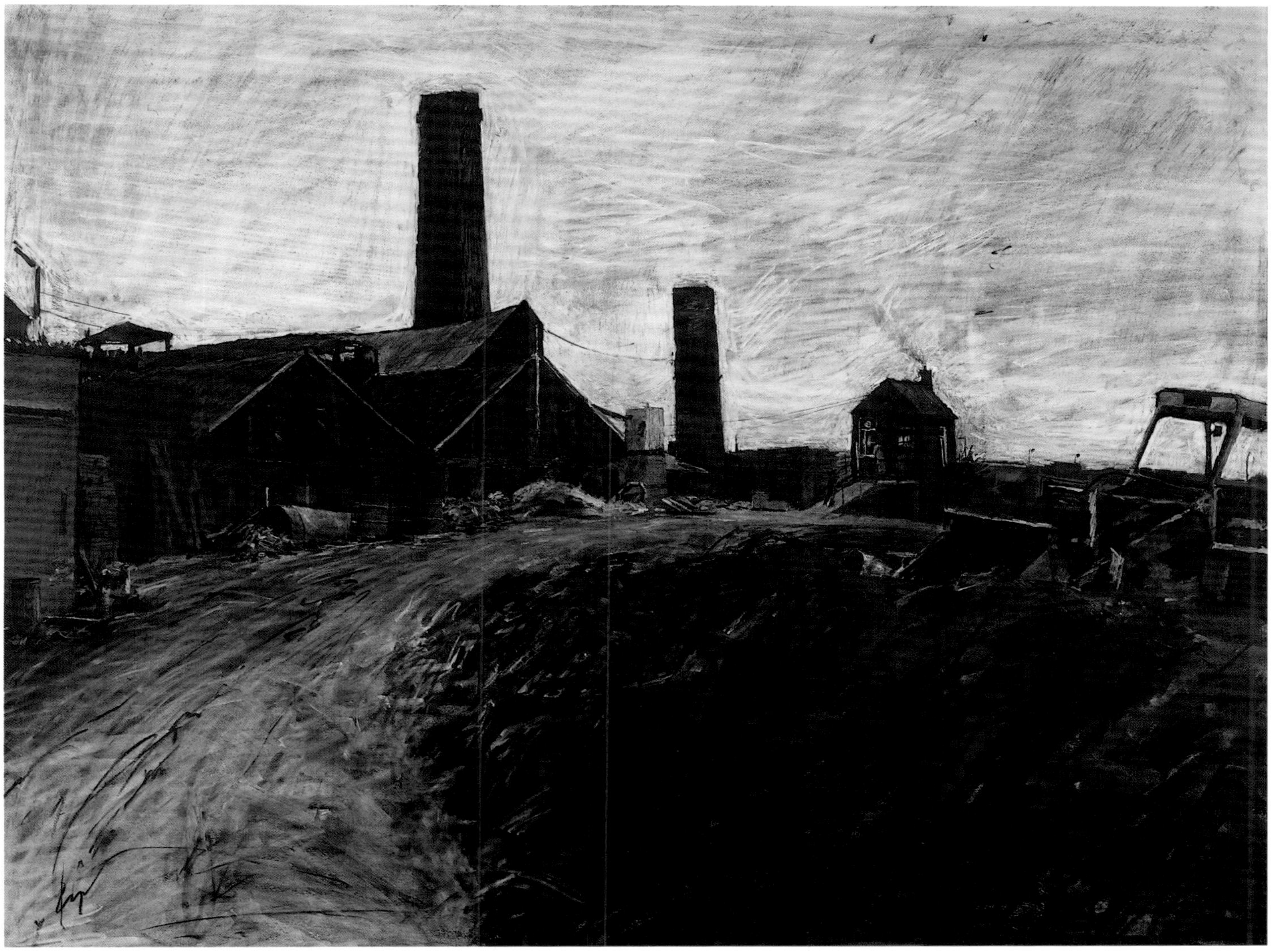

Wild and windy, sitting down in the gutter, Boulby. March 1973. Charcoal, pencil & Conté. 20″×30″.

Lower. Exterior of Blythe's Best Brickworks, Washington, three o'clock by the office clock. 1977. Charcoal, pencil & Conté. 29″×39″.

There were projects working in the ironworks at Teeside, where he spent nights working in the heat and dust, excited by the flow and drama of the glow of molten iron. He would drive home in the early hours so exalted that he would go straight out to make drawings of freshly fallen snow. Such contrasts of environment have been important to Len. Man in his workplace confronting and challenging nature; whether it be in the sea, the steelworks or the Potash mine; all have been significant, atmosphere has been important. Perhaps his preoccupation with details, such as the girders of the tunnel supports, holding up the roof in the Potash mine, might be seen as a distraction from seemingly more spiritual things, but in these drawings he shows his interest in engineering and architecture. Still, in the very dark black drawings of the mine, there is a great feeling of the infinite and the uncertain, the very thing that makes mining such a precarious occupation. There are the glimpses of miners moving in and out of the darkness. Figure drawing in the landscape is difficult, and even more difficult at the bottom of the mine. These drawings were not made in the studio, they are real, they were made from miners in working conditions. Art is Len's last consideration, the works are made out of respect and curiosity, and as honestly as Len's talent will allow.

There are no pretensions about this work, simply a celebration of Len's fascination with nature and his compulsion to do everything to the best of his ability.

Over the years the house has grown and expanded, so has his family, now five children in all. Also the geese, the ducks and the vegetables, in whose production all the family are involved. For the present it is Len that makes the drawings but he thrives on the support of his family, his wife Helen in particular. It is not coincidence that over the years, as the family responsibility grows and the security with it, so the work has become more spontaneous and richer in colour and light. Gone is the austerity of the early days, there is a greater sense of energy and a more joyous celebration of the sea and its battle with the land.

To write about the practicalities of Len's method of working at the sea's edge and sometimes in it, will only support romantic notions, but of course the sea is romantic, why else do people gaze from the shore out to the horizon if it is not to dream? It is not just the water itself, a river is different. To stand and look out across the sea, to see the shimmer of light, suggests travel and adventure. The sea, for the lone Atlantic sailor or the old age pensioner dipping his toes, has a magic and mystery of its own. Len's work fits into this tradition, he has worked from the cliff top, from the edge of the sea and most recently out in the North Sea itself.

These paintings and drawings of Len Tabner's are not about deciding 'Is it Great?' or 'Is it Art?' Such notions would not come into his thinking, and in any case time itself takes care of such things. The work is about one person with talent and need, simply using it to the full, in the best way that he can, to be part of nature and not just an observer.

Peter Prendergast
July 1989

Peter Prendergast is a painter living in North Wales. He was born in Abertridwr South Wales, where his father was a miner.

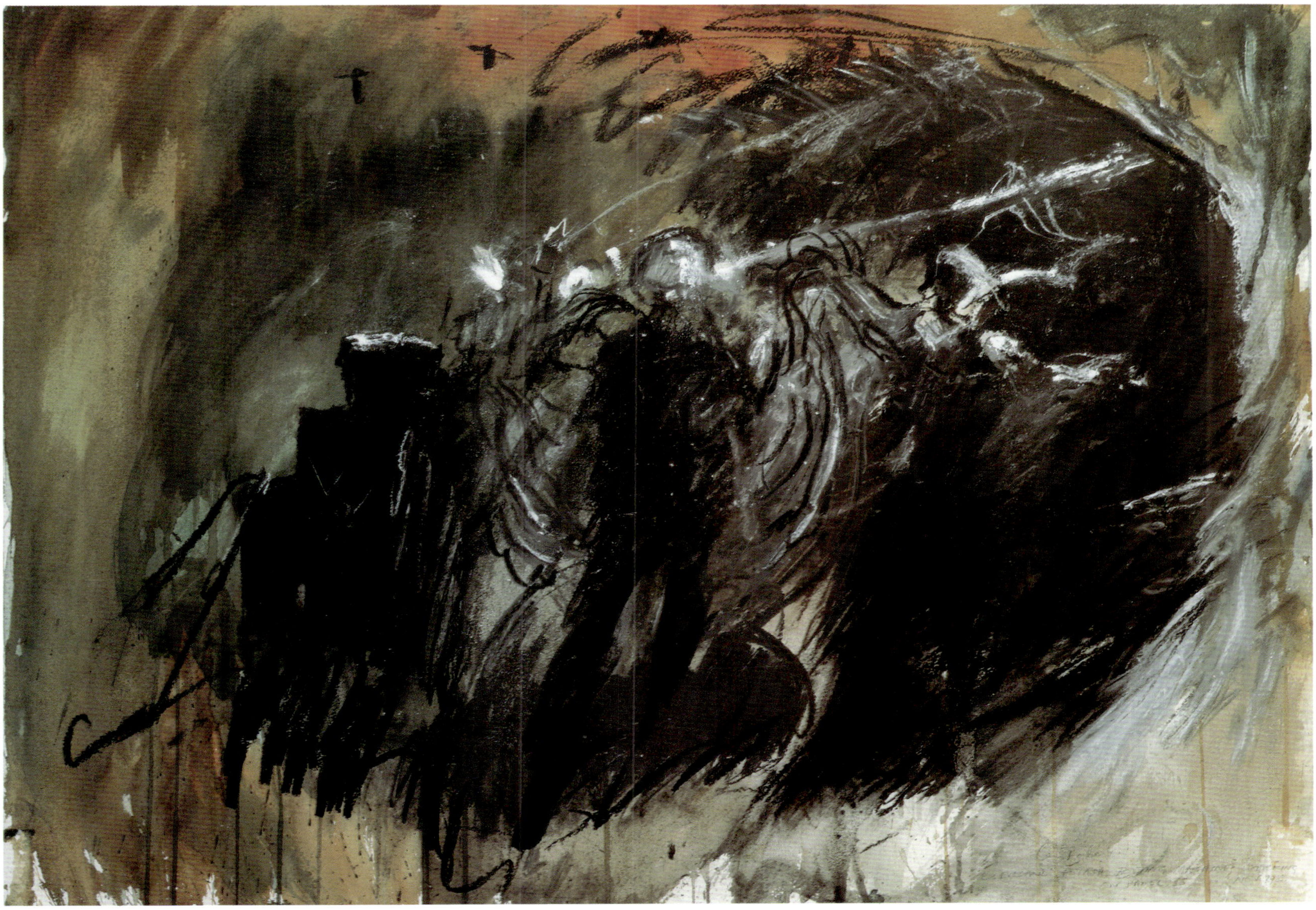

Miners working at the face, panel 35, operating bolting machine. Cleveland Potash Mine November 1983.
Watercolour and pastel on hand made paper. 22″×31″.

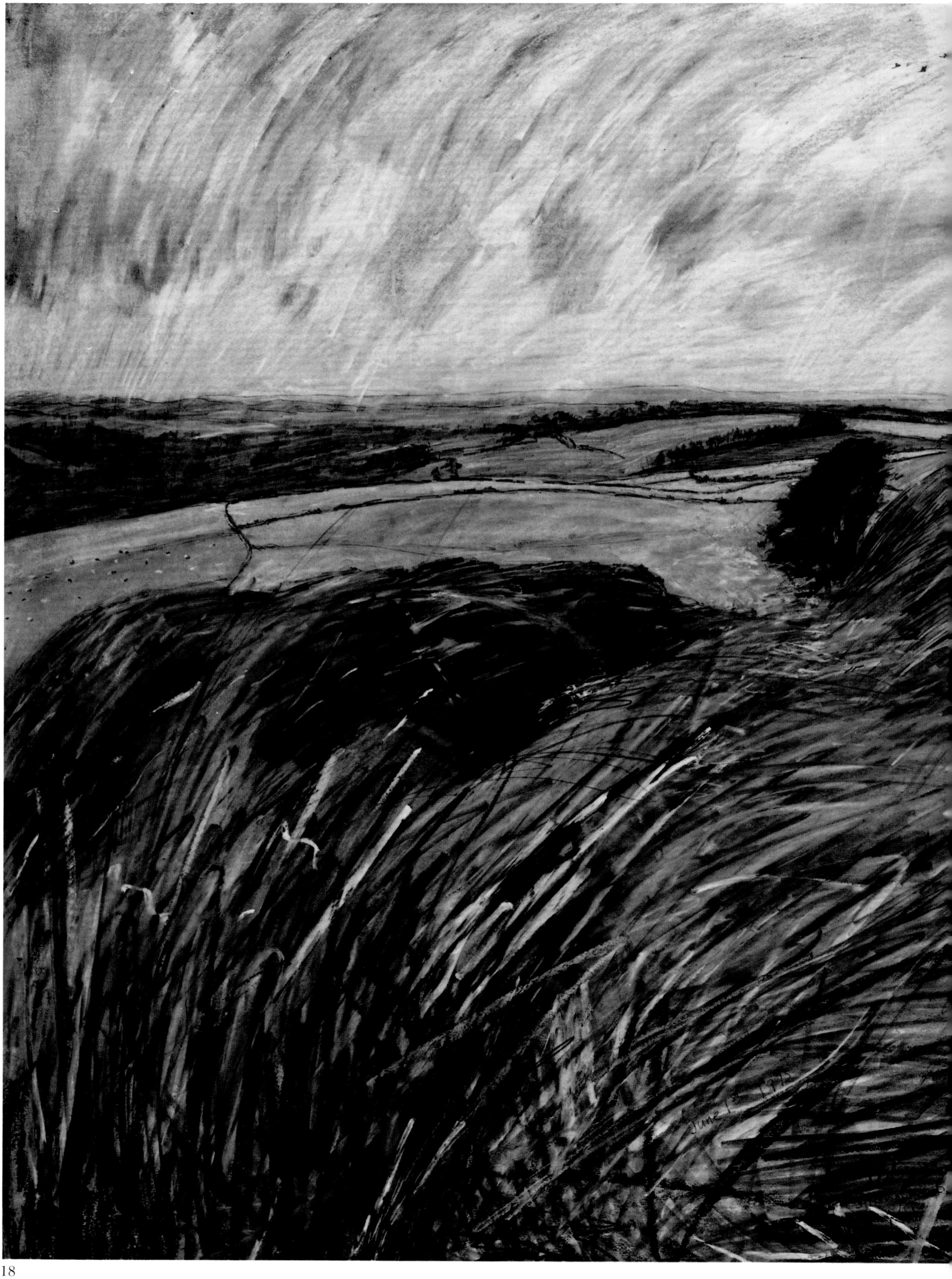

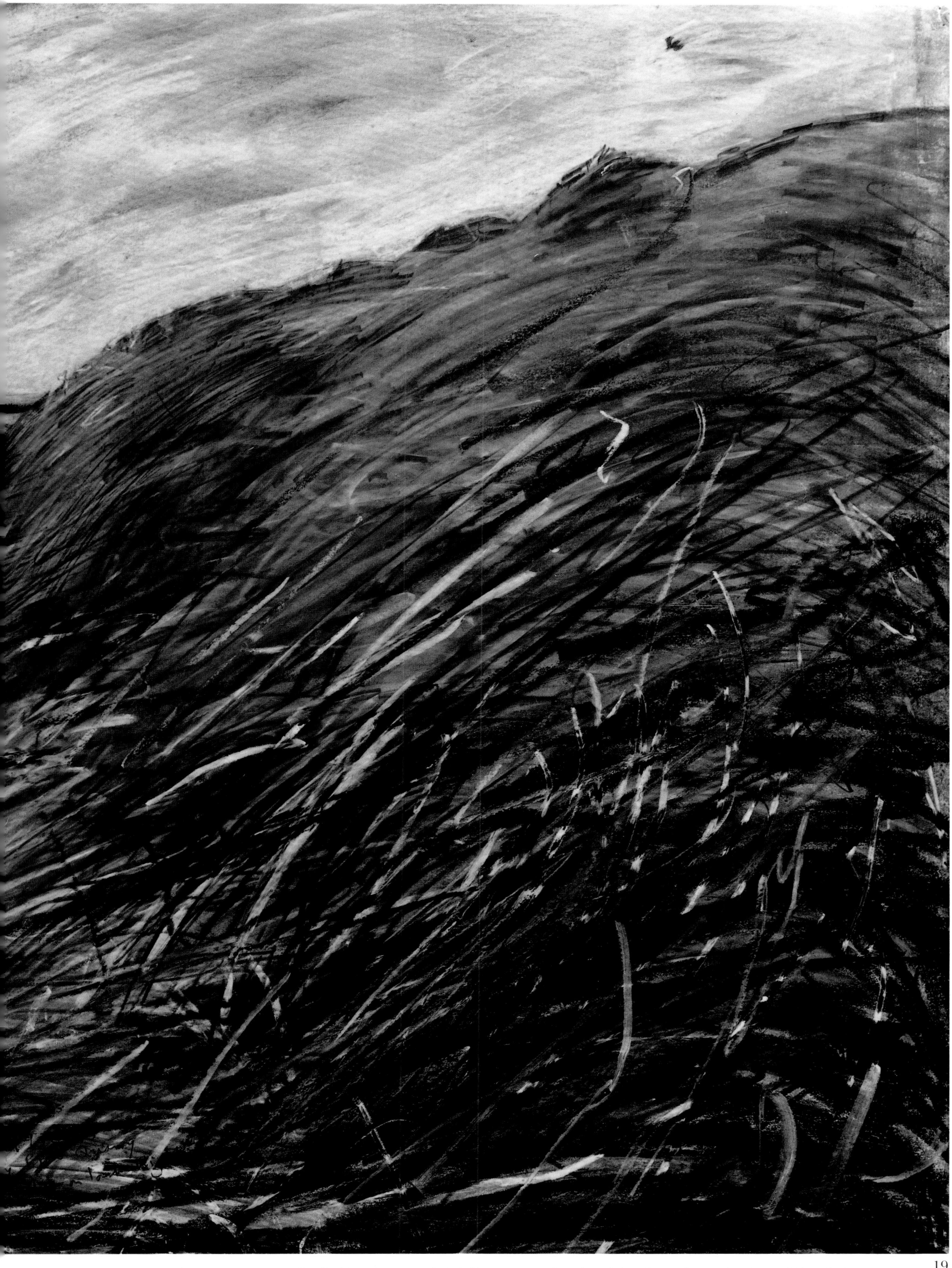

Sitting in Bank Brow Quarry, Boulby, looking over towards Grinkle, not as windy as last night. Charcoal, pencil & Conté. 20″×30″ 1972.

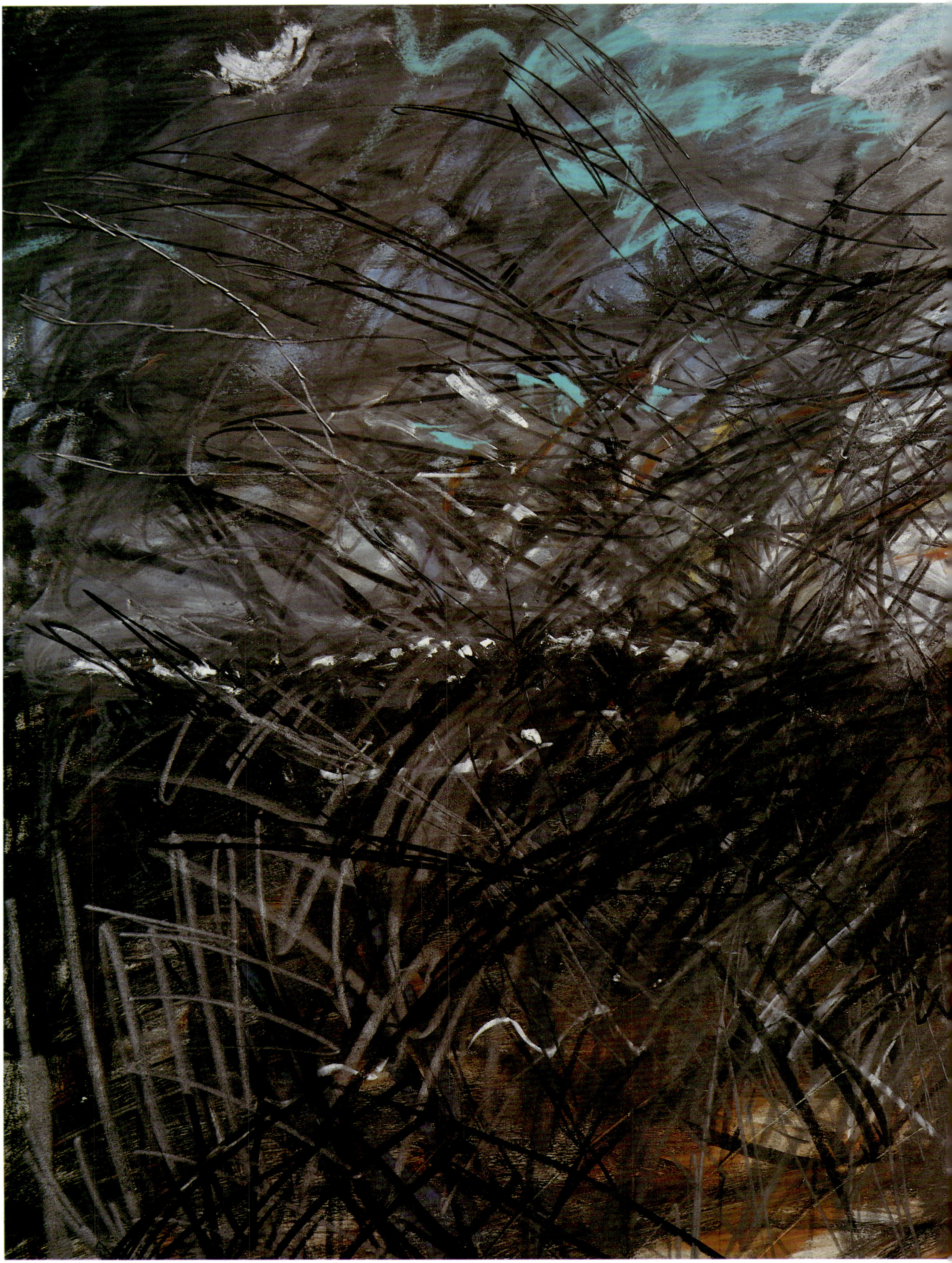

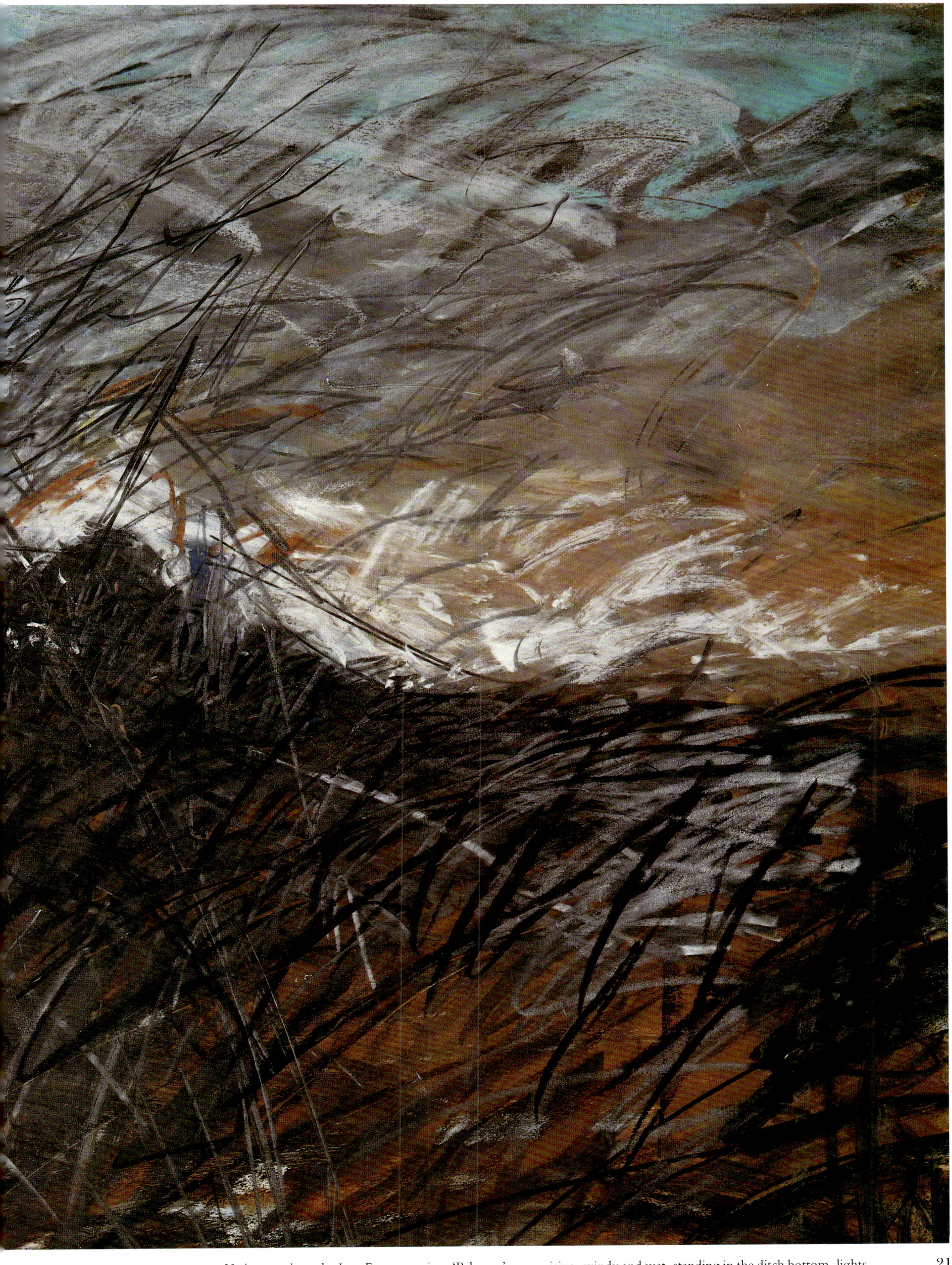

Hedgerow down by Ings Farm, evening, 'Palmery' moon rising, windy and wet, standing in the ditch bottom, lights showing over towards East Loftus, March 1981. Watercolour, Charcoal pencil and pastel. 29″×39″.

Hawthorn hedge, wet thundery afternoon, Boulby. Watercolour 1980. Approximately 12″×12″. Private collection.

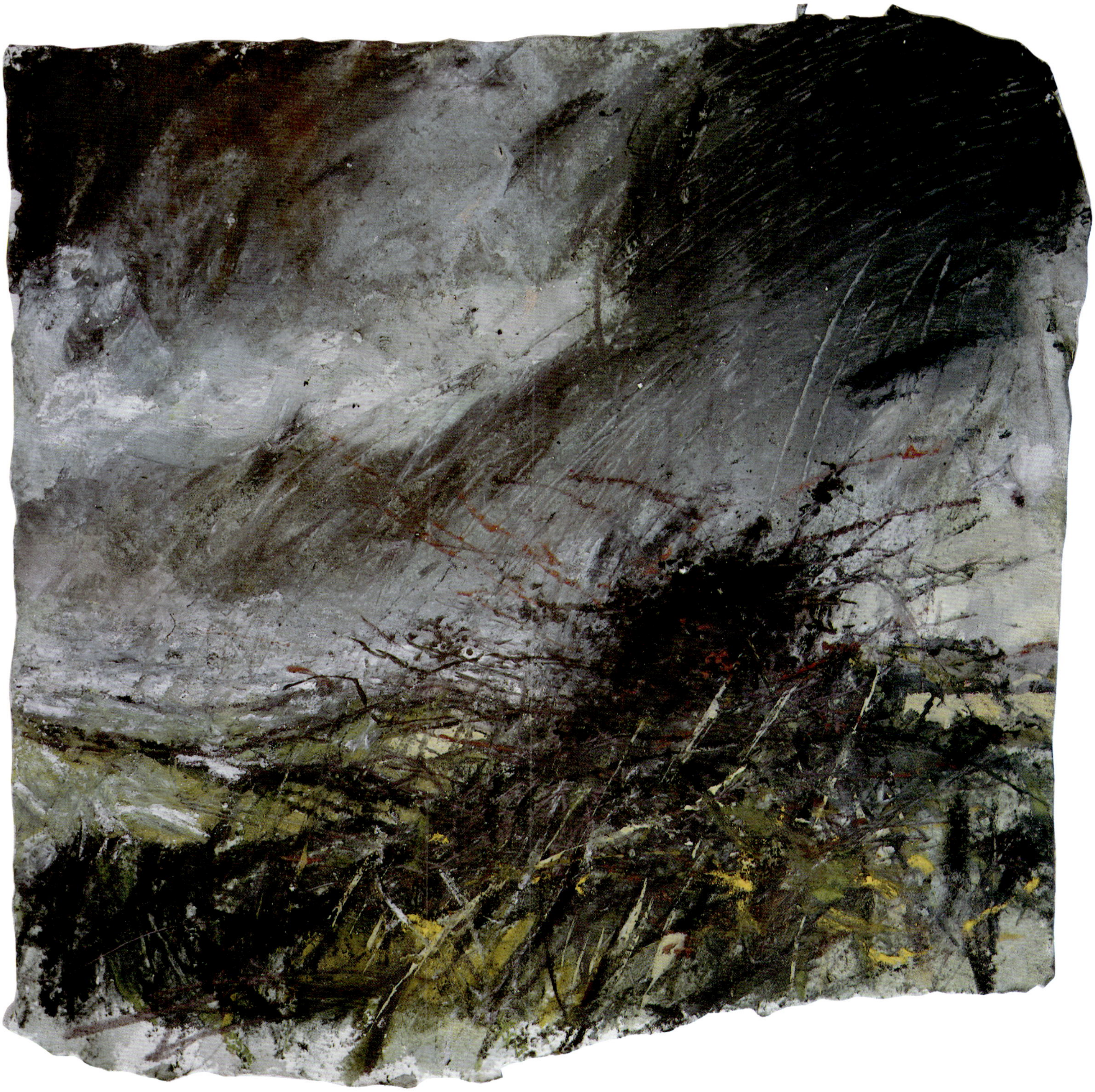

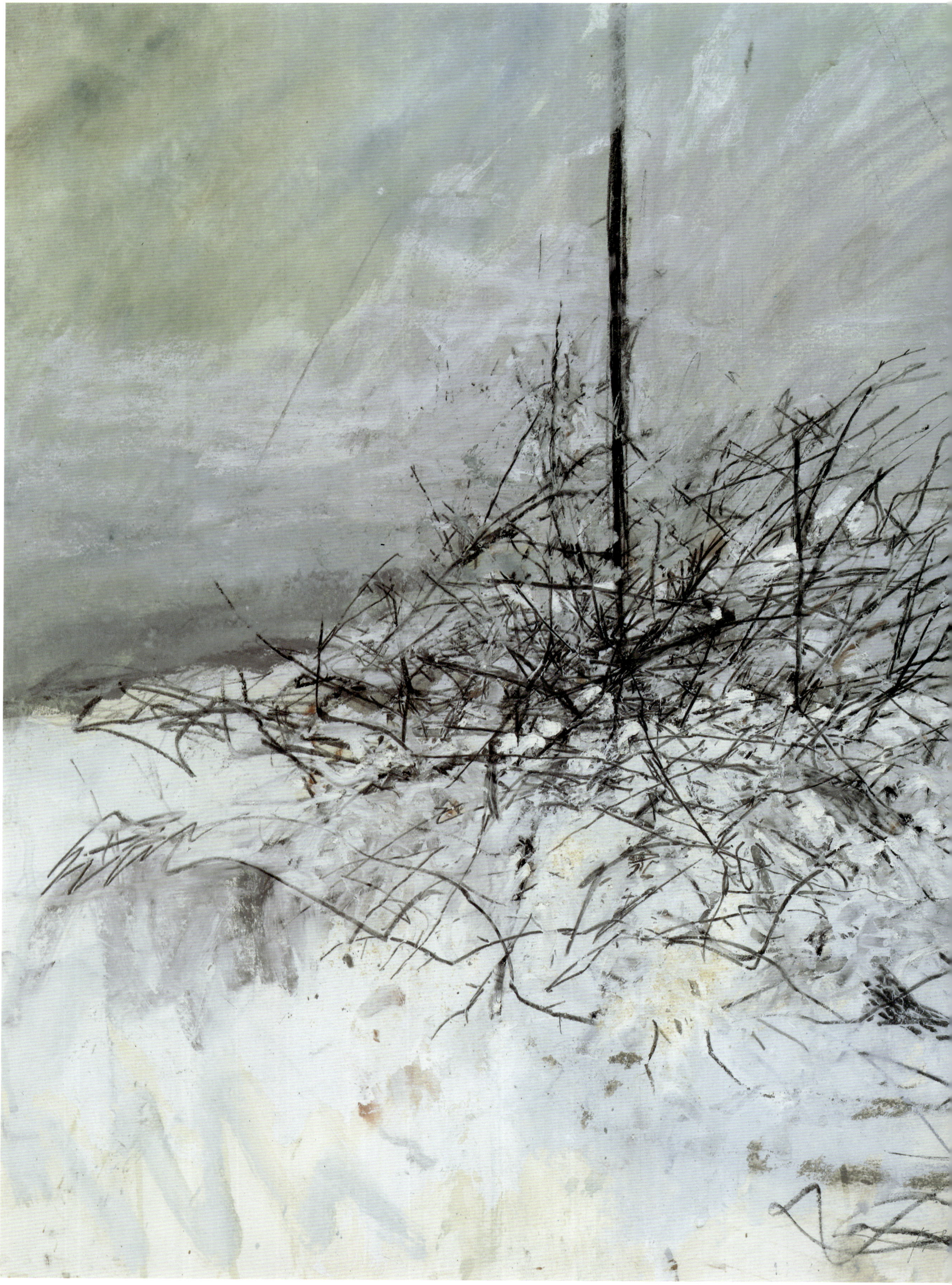

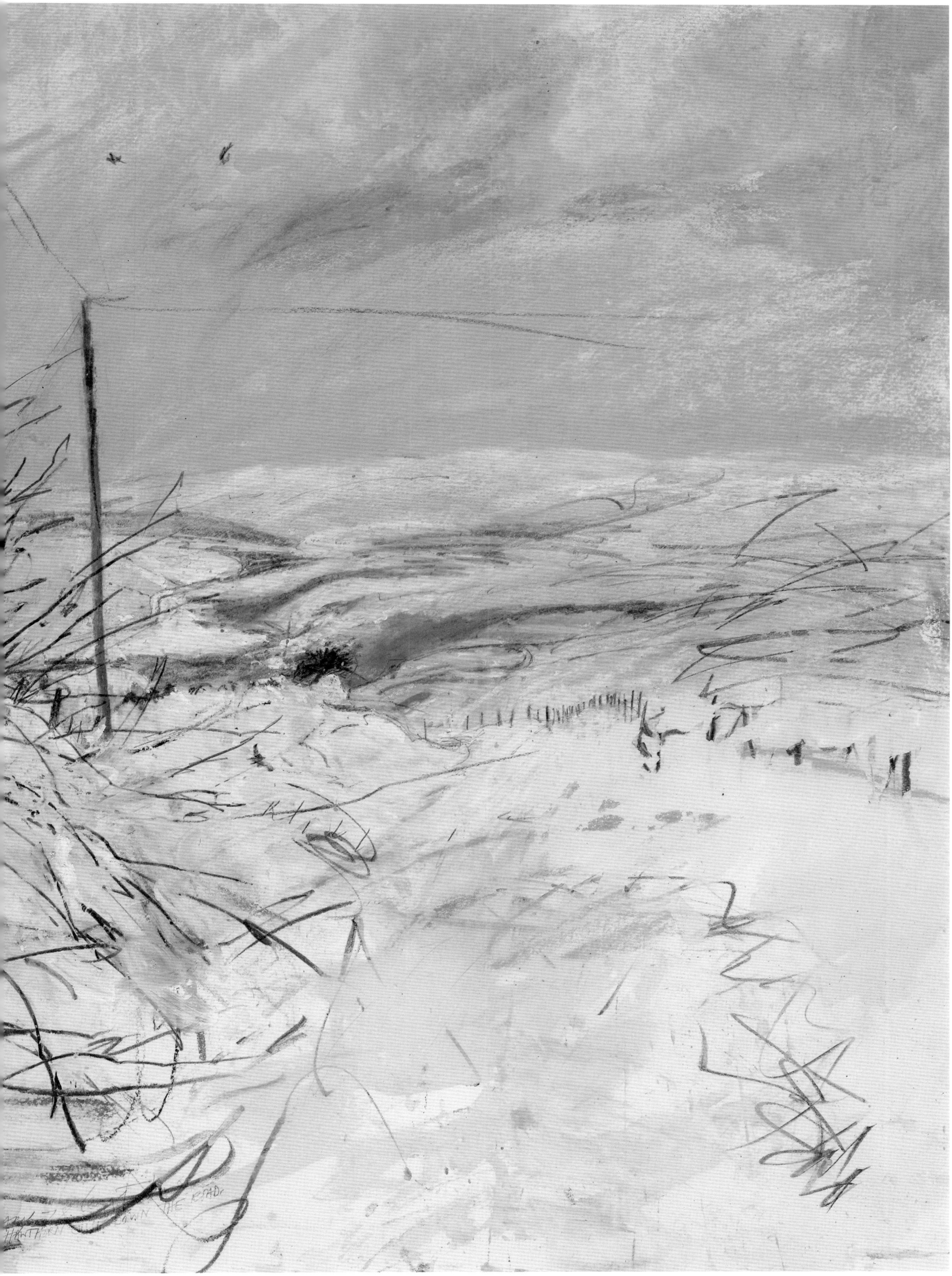

Hawthorn just down the road, deepish snow February 1978. Watercolour & pencil. 22″×30″.

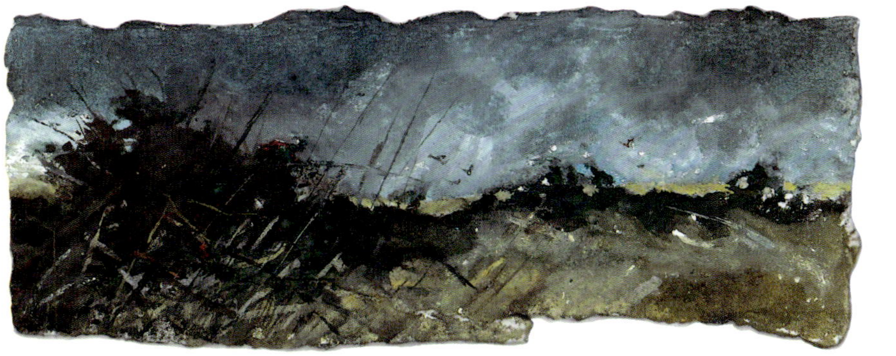

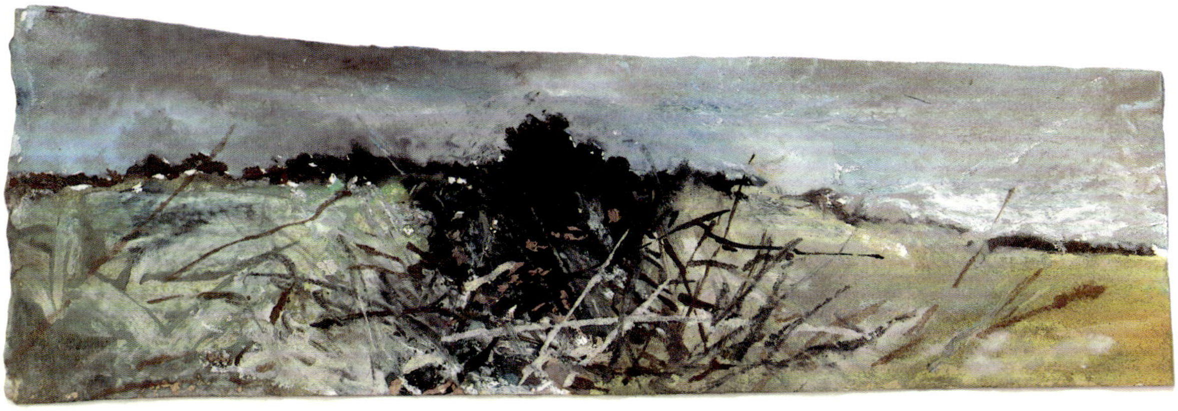

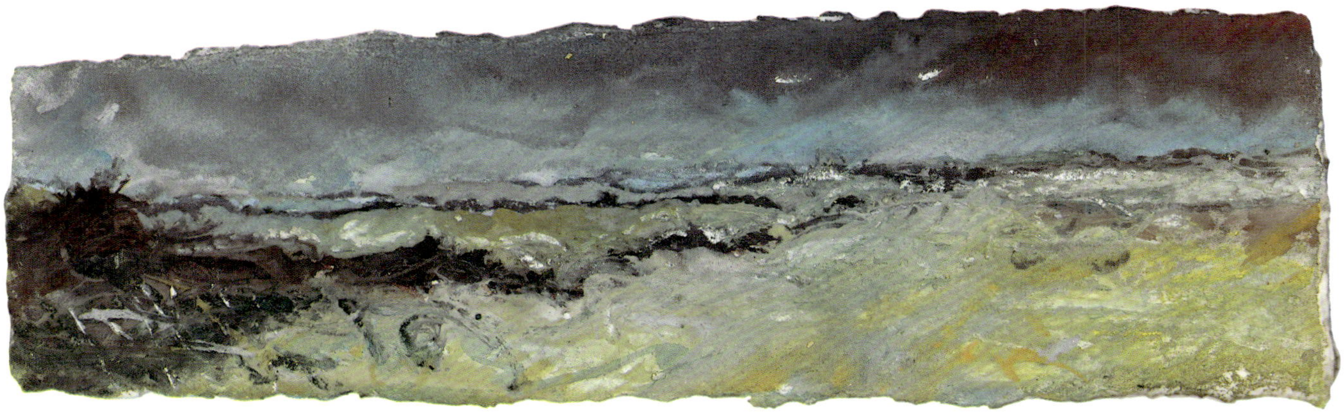

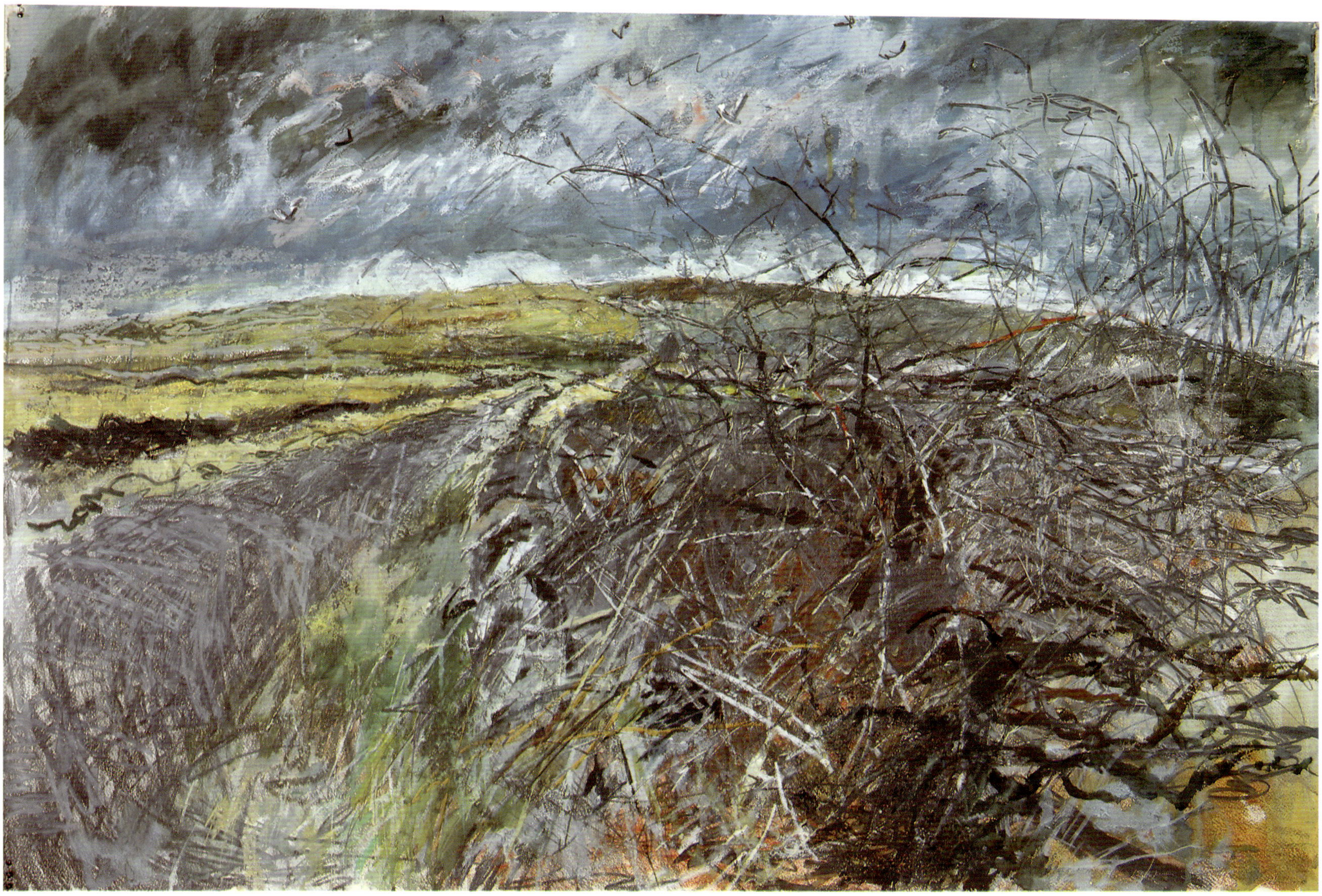

Looking up towards Boulby, from the end of Micklow Lane December 1977–January 1978. Watercolour, pastel & Graphite. 27½″×41″.

Hawthorn hedges, three studies of field corners Boulby, summer 1981. Watercolour on fragments of handmade paper, actual size.

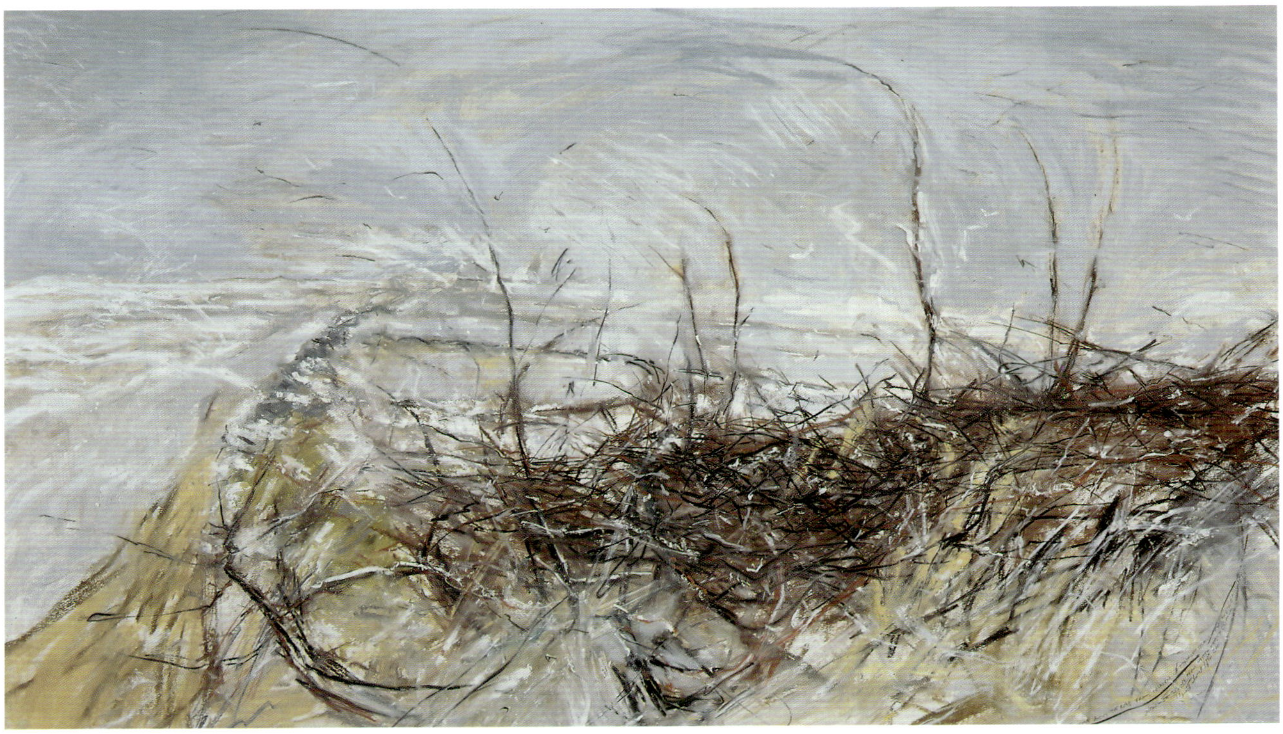

Break between heavy driving snowstorms, hawthorn at the roadside, end of Micklow Lane. February 1983. Watercolour 28″×50″. Darlington Art Gallery.

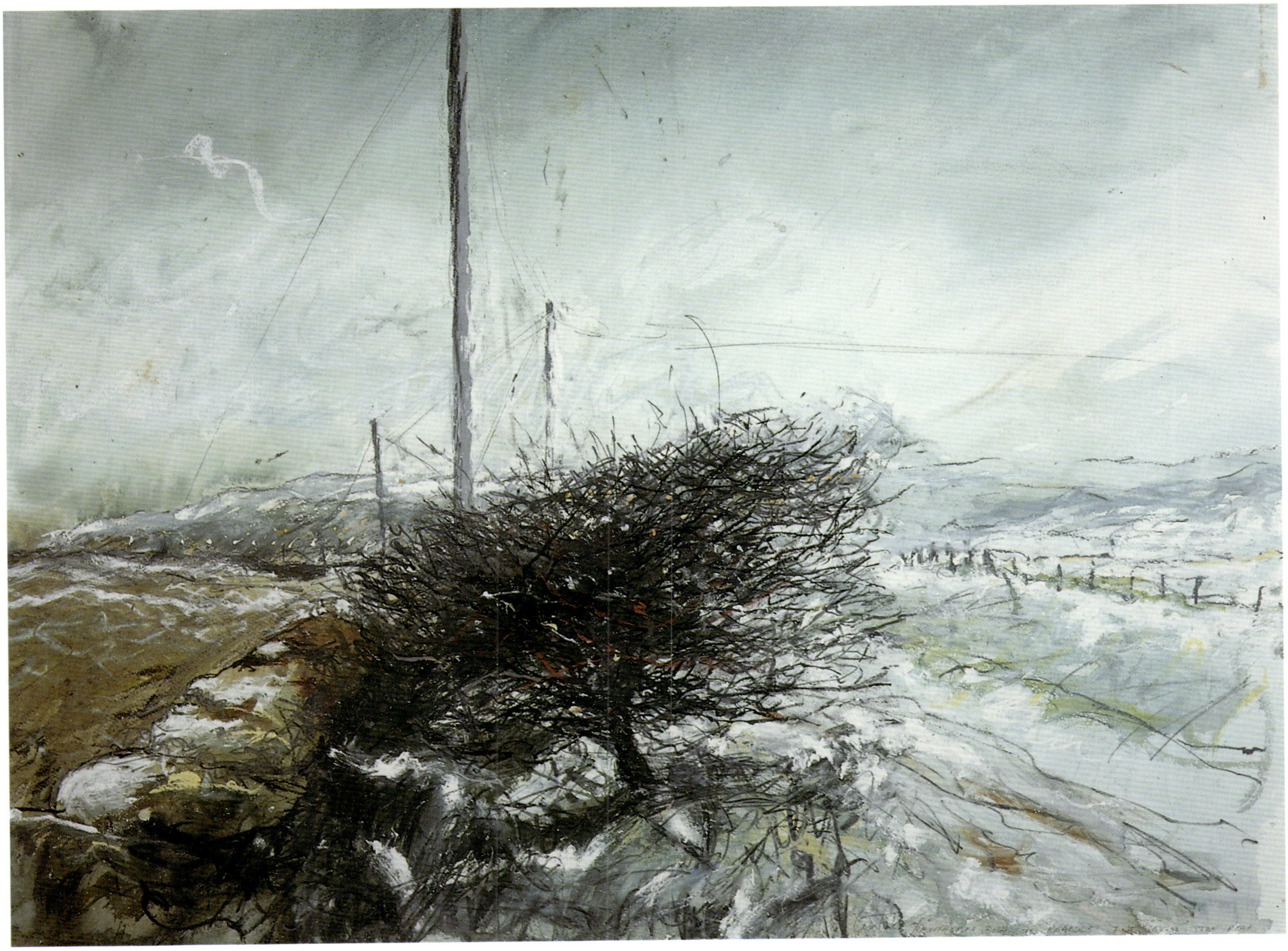

Hawthorn at the roadside, just down the road from the house, February 1983, snow lying, watercolour 22″×31″. Private collection.

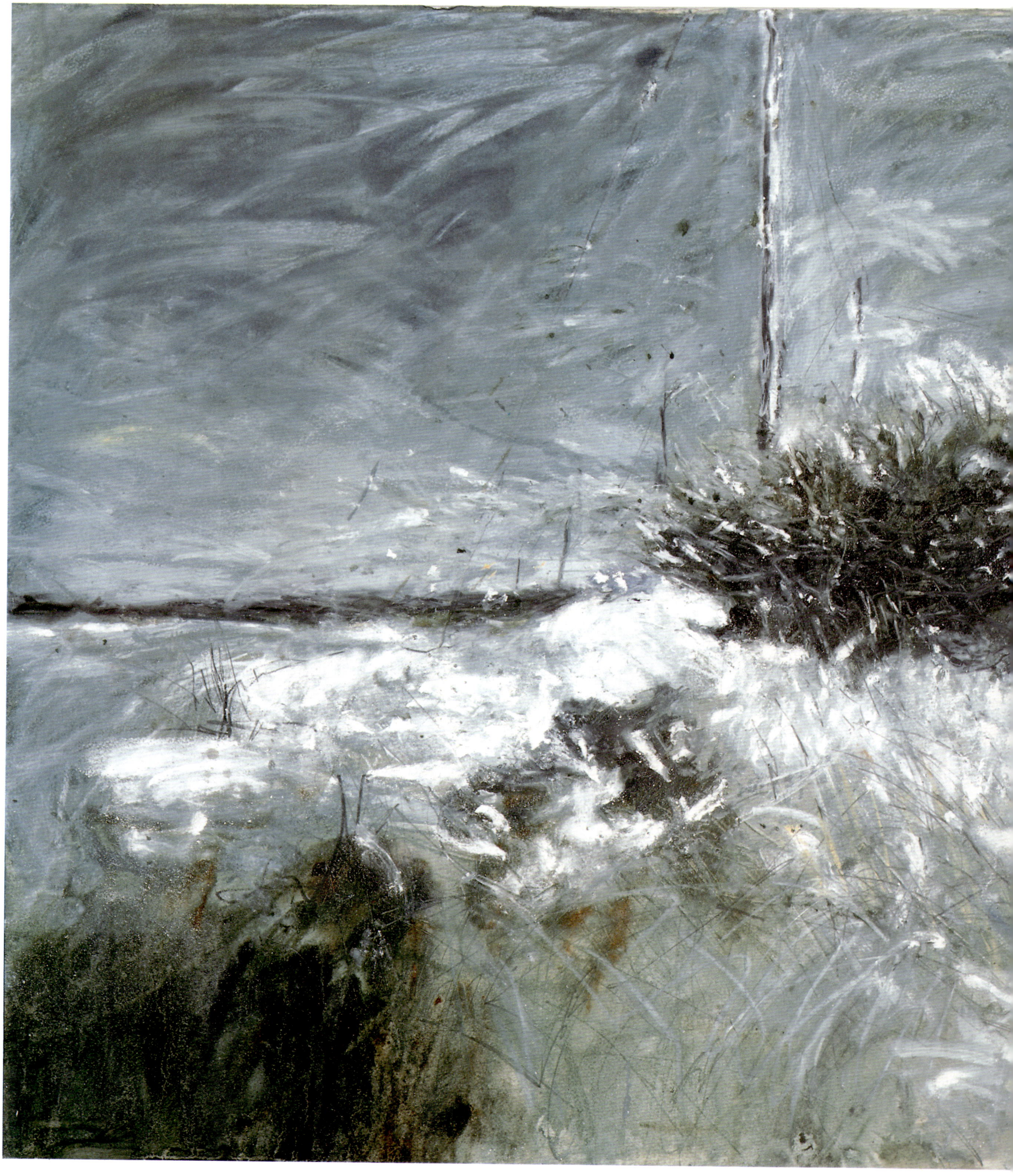

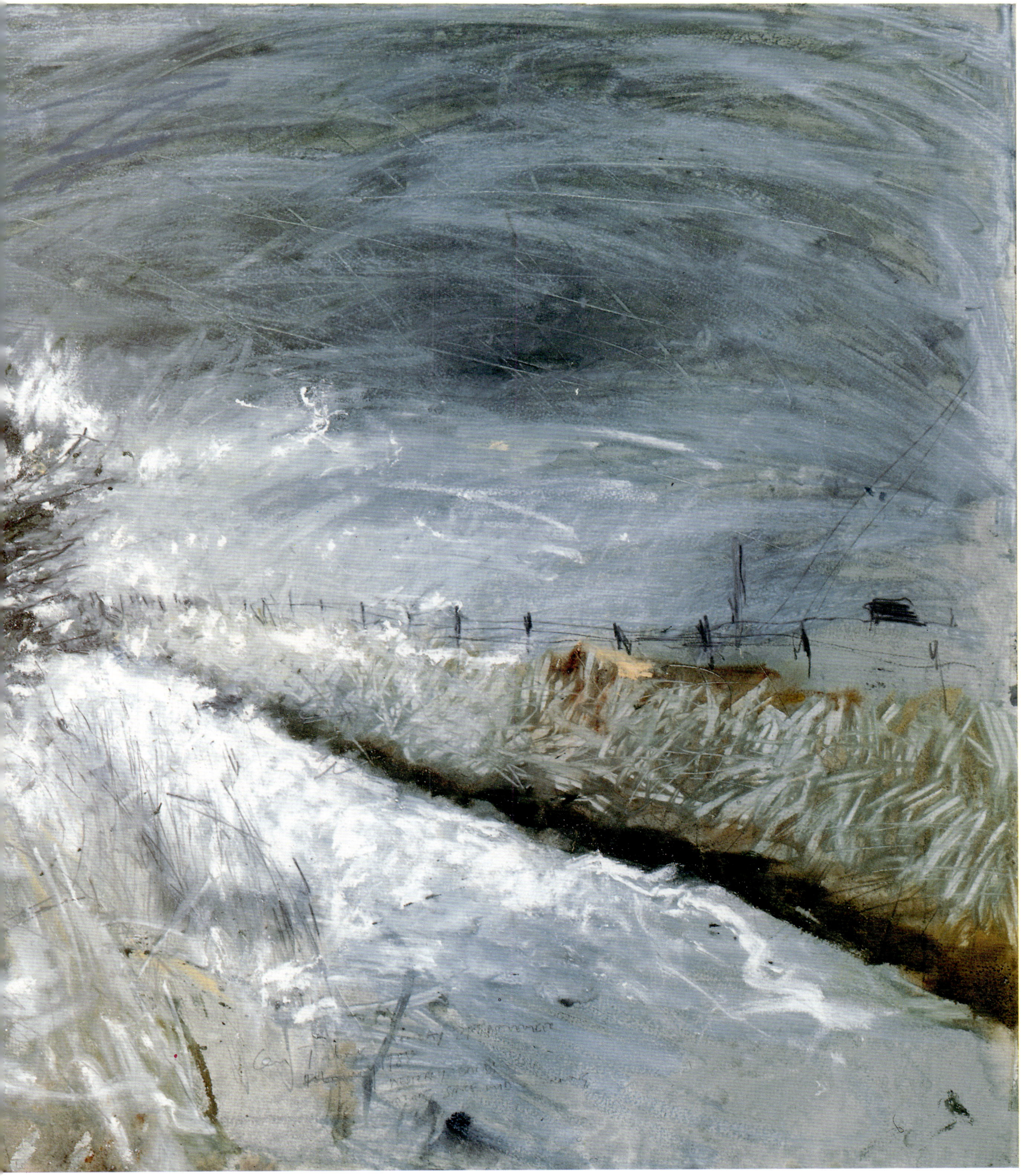

Monday 21st November 1988, westerly winds, snowing since mid-morning. Watercolour & pastel. 32″×54″.

Working in the fields close by my home, with the wind fresh and the air, perhaps cold and damp, or even snow laden, I am aware that 4,000 feet beneath me, men are working in heat and noise, dryness and dust.

The idea of human activity almost a mile down beneath my studio, beneath my kitchen floor, in the darkness of rocks laid down 240 million years ago, intrigued and fascinated me to the extent that eventually I felt that I must go down and be there, watching, exploring and in some small way even taking part in the activity itself.

I first went down into the mine in 1982 after trying many times to get access to draw and paint. I was staggered by how different it was to what I had expected. The mine is a relatively new one, it did not exist in 1969 when I moved to live in Boulby, and yet everything seemed so corroded and antiquated, the corrosion itself caused by the existence of beds of salt immediately beneath the potash. The tunnels or roadways, cavernous and massive, the sides apparently disintegrating and collapsing, the roof held up by bolts and strapping, cables and pipes slung from hooks on the walls and roof slabs, and above all the darkness. In my naivity I had expected concrete lined access ways, neat little railways and lighting, at least in working areas. I was soon "put right" by Steve Maxwell, the mine manager, who showed me round on my first day. The walls needed to collapse, he explained, in order to let the roof slab come down in a controlled way so that the immense pressure of 4,000 feet of rock overhead could be relieved. In fact the walls are purposely weakened to encourage their collapse. Lighting is virtually non-existent because there are miles of roadways and the cost would be prohibitive, instead men wear cap lamps and the mining machines carry their own headlamps, usually dust covered and glowering in the darkness as they whine towards you. Transport is by conveyor. All this added, to what was for me the richness and wonder of a whole new world. It was as if I had suddenly been transported to live at the bottom of the sea. Everything seemed so magic and totally different, and potentially dangerous.

The heat and dryness of the air, combined with the feeling of pressure on my ears, made breathing and walking both exhausting and difficult. It was a long time before I became acclimatised and able to overcome the feelings of lethargy and weariness I experienced every time I went down the shaft.

To begin with I was escorted everywhere by one of the miners, after about a week, however, I was able to come and go quite freely and explore alone – sit and think in odd dark corners, watch and absorb the things about me. Gradually I became aware of the things which I felt I needed to work from, the aspects of the mine which moved and excited me the most. I was often torn between two opposing aspects, the need to describe, to work descriptively and convey the exactness of the structure, the massiveness of the machinery, the cavernousness of the spaces, but also, and often conflicting with this, the need even greater, to say something about the unknown and the mysterious. Groups of figures moving, half seen in the darkness. The void and emptiness of some of the tunnels, the oppressive heat and stale air, to say something of the weariness, the sheer physical exhaustion of the work the men were doing. The way conveyors carrying potash, or travelling empty, or even conveying recumbent miners into or out from, the face areas – run seemingly into the very bowels of the earth. And even sadly and most unsuccessfully to express something of the tension and pain and suffering, when on two occasions whilst I was working, roof falls caused fatal accidents – being part of the roll call of assembled men with drawn faces waiting at the pit head for news of men trapped below. News that they knew full well could only be what they did not wish to hear.

On and off I worked for over two years painting, drawing, watching, underground – sometimes almost daily or nightly for weeks on end, at other times spasmodically underground one day, out on the shore the next. A beginning has been made, I feel there is much more to say and I must return.

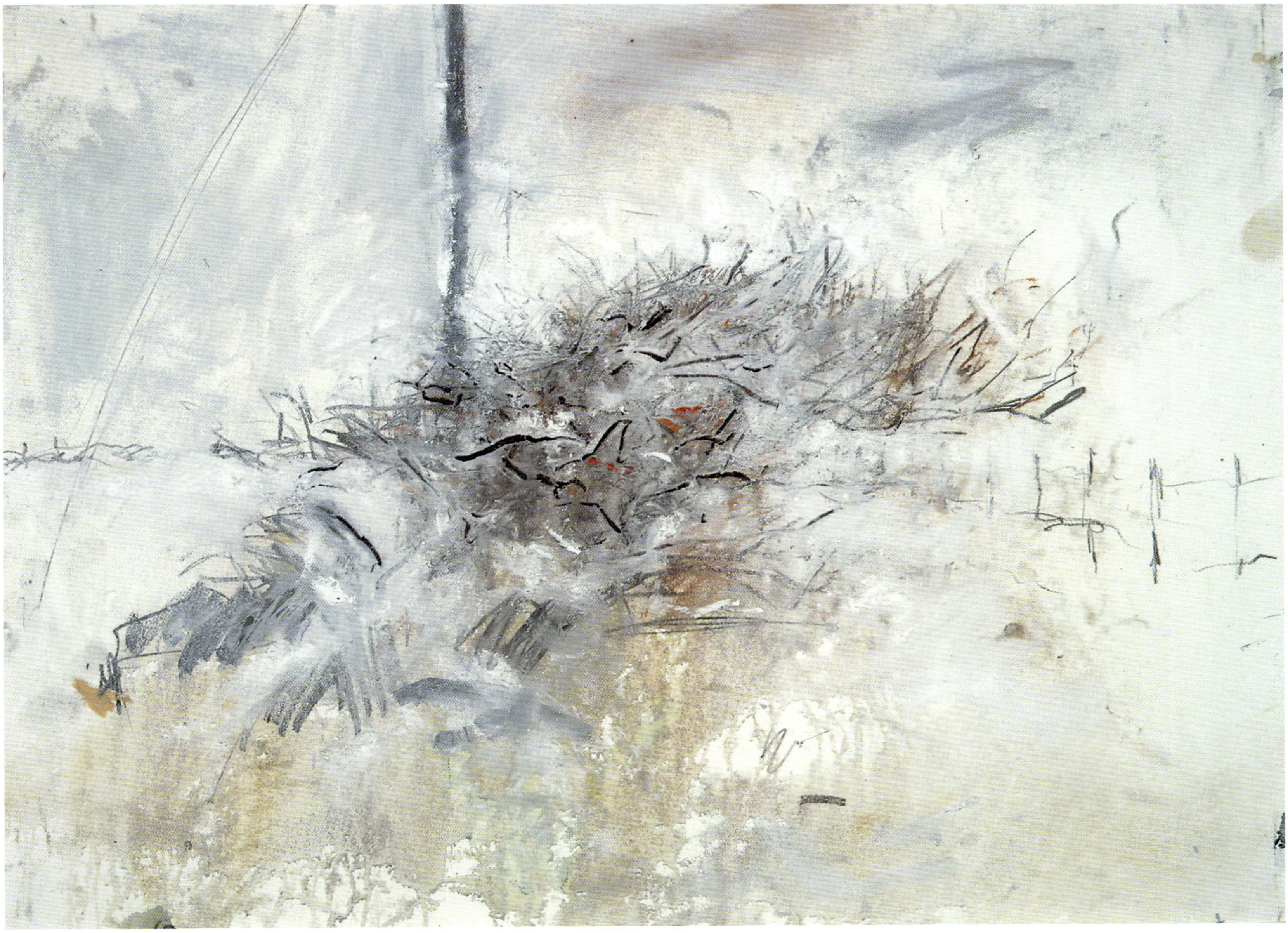

Hawthorn in snow, very heavy snowstorm. Watercolour, pastel, graphite & oil pastel. 22″×31″.

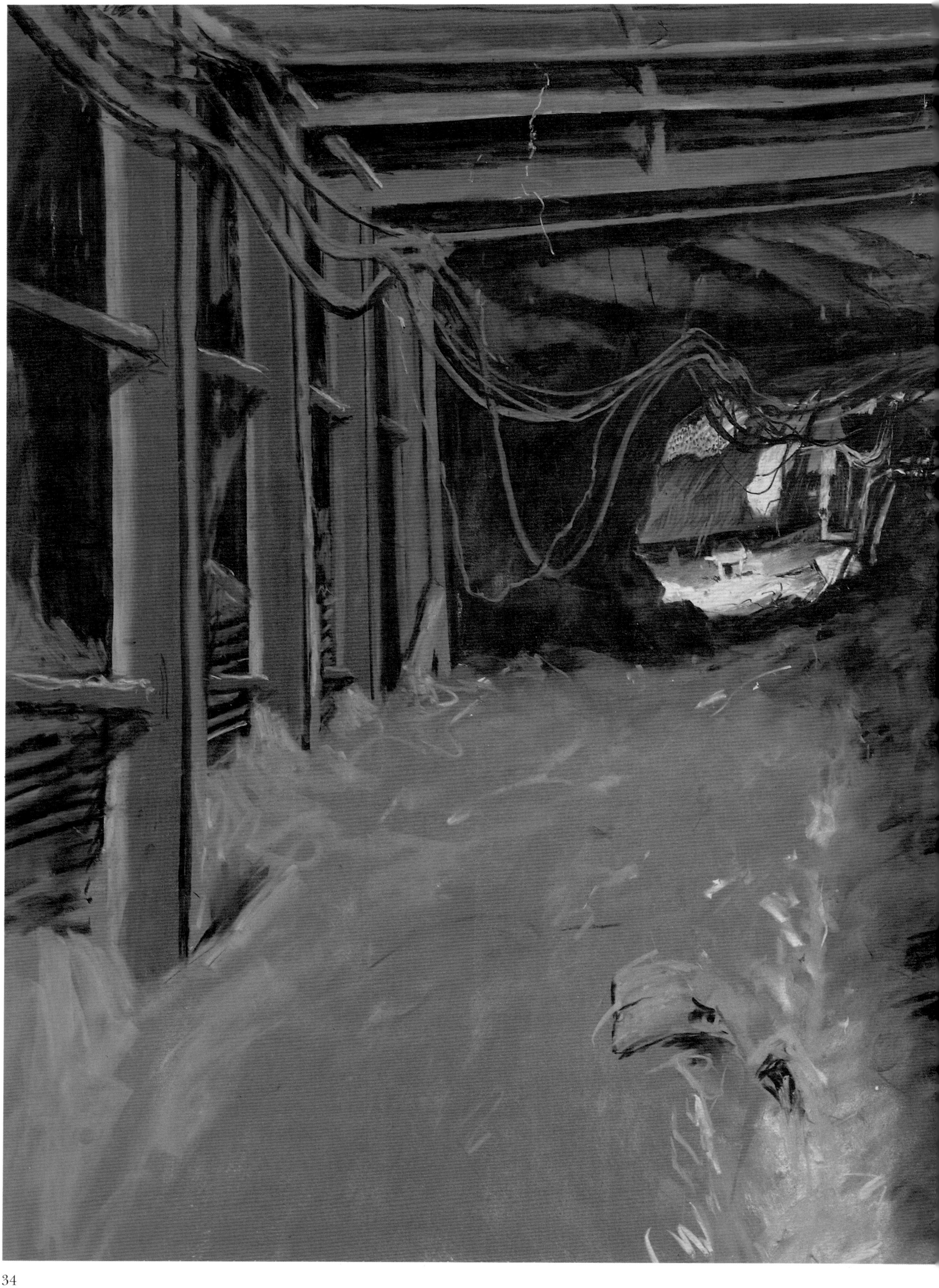

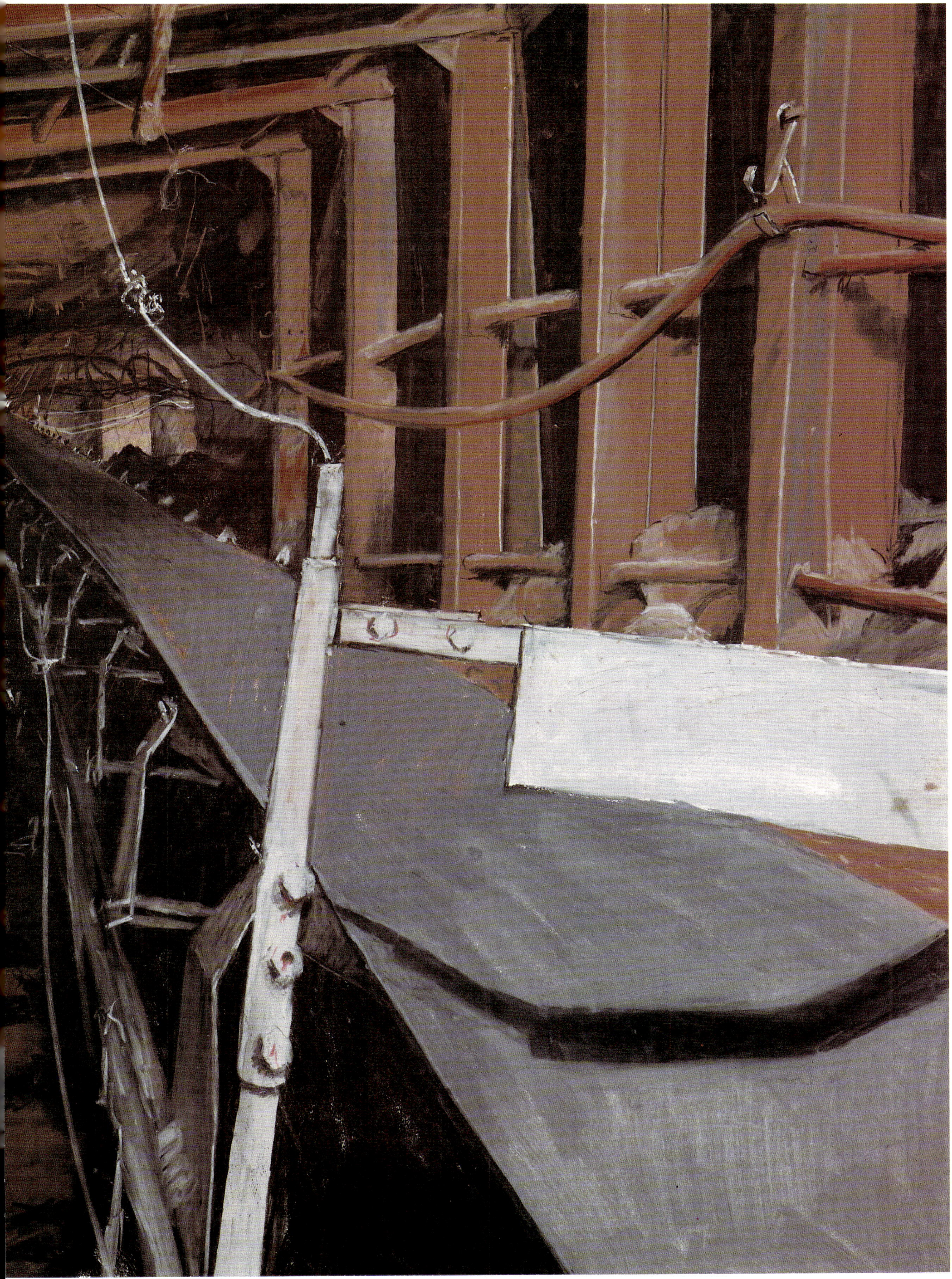

Cleveland Potash Mine, man saving gate, 5.1 belt, near belt end, just before 60″ belt. Control room down on the left, side walls and roof slab supported by heavy girders, buckling due to pressure. November 1983. Charcoal & Conté. 30″×40″. Science Museum, London

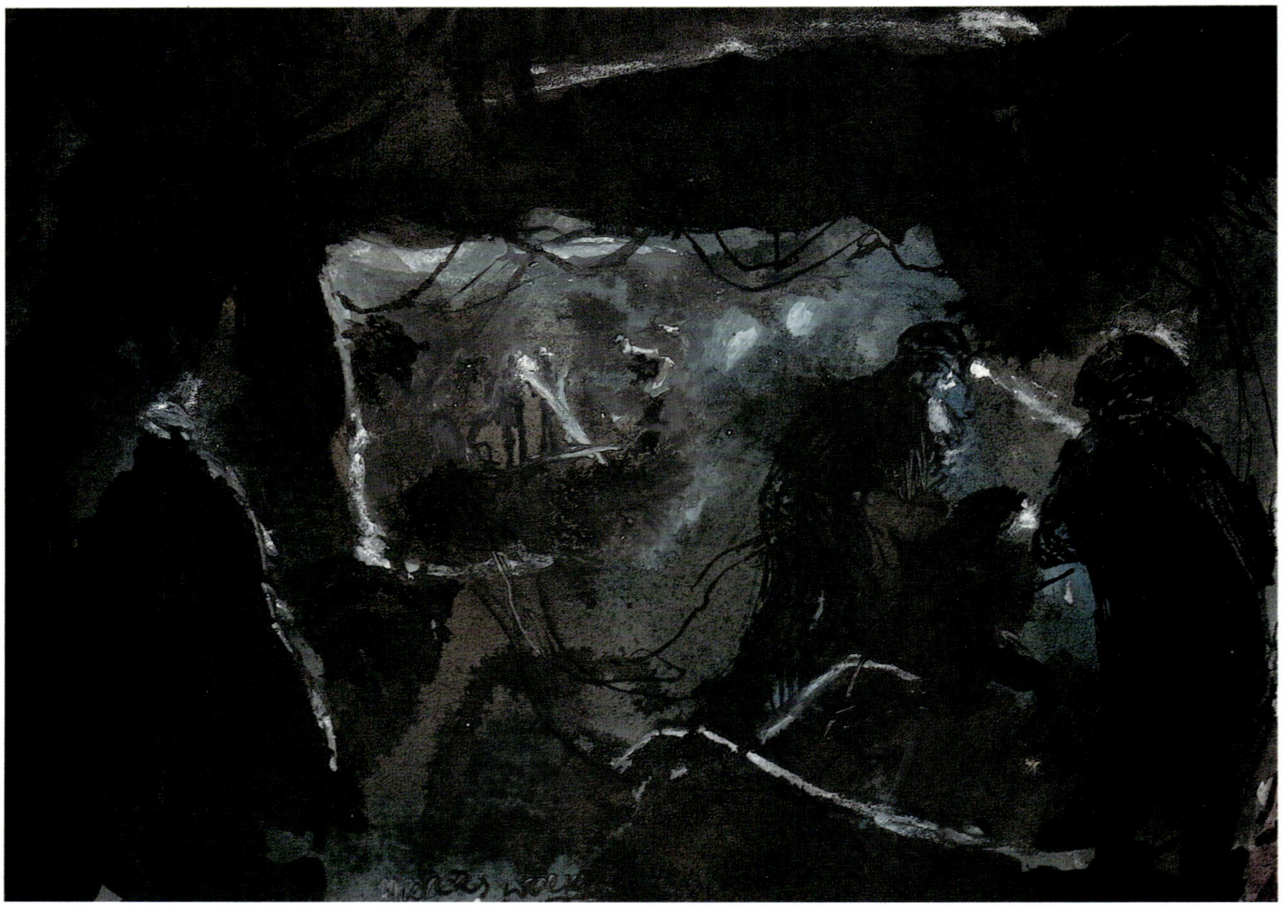

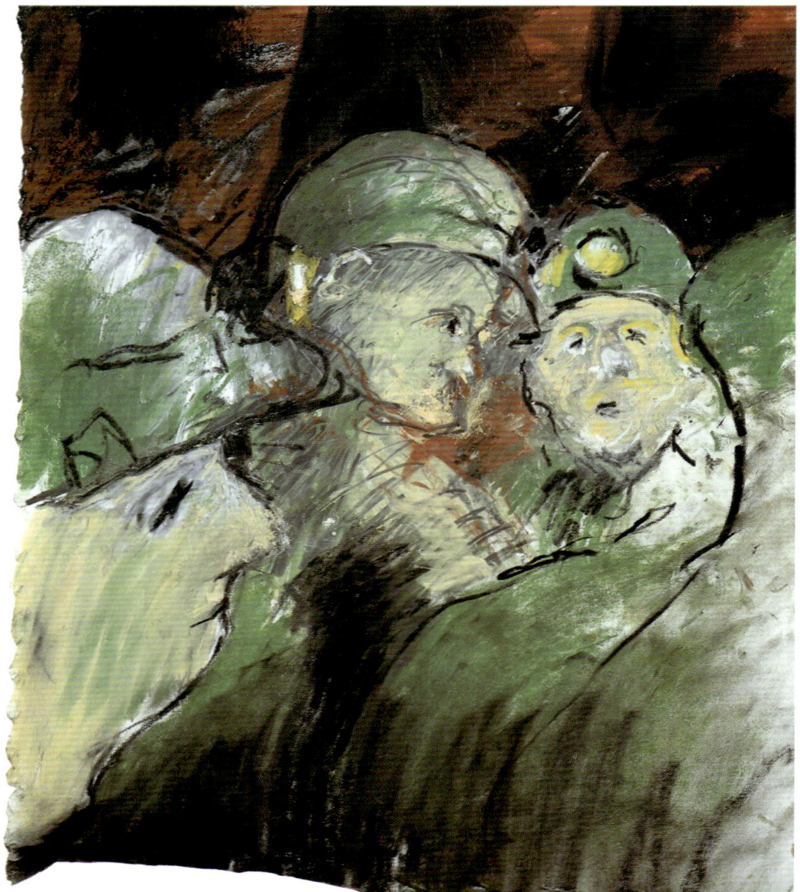

Miners working at the face No. 35 panel. Ink.

Lower. In the cage – "Move over a bit mate an' make some room." Pastel, torn fragment. Private collection.

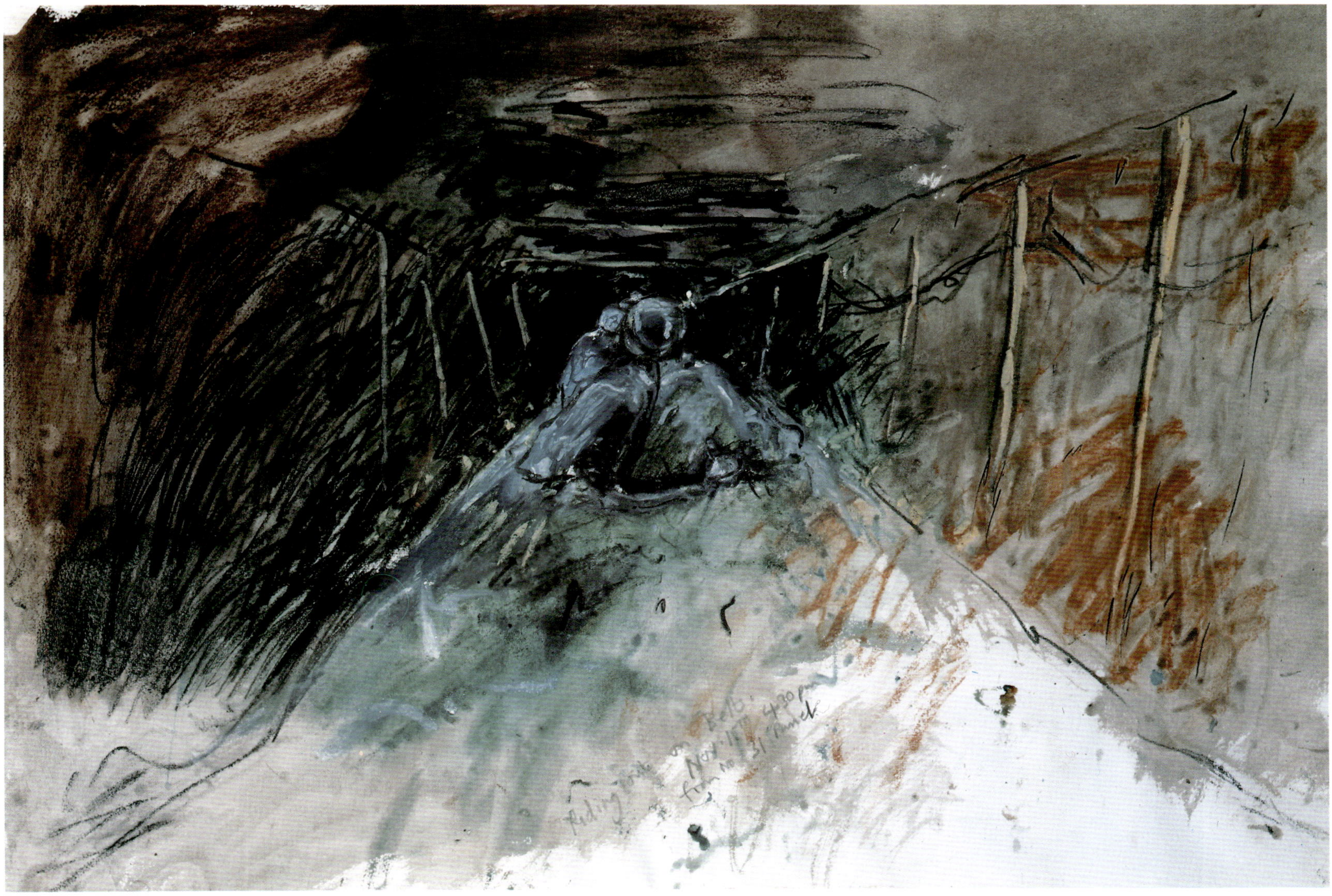

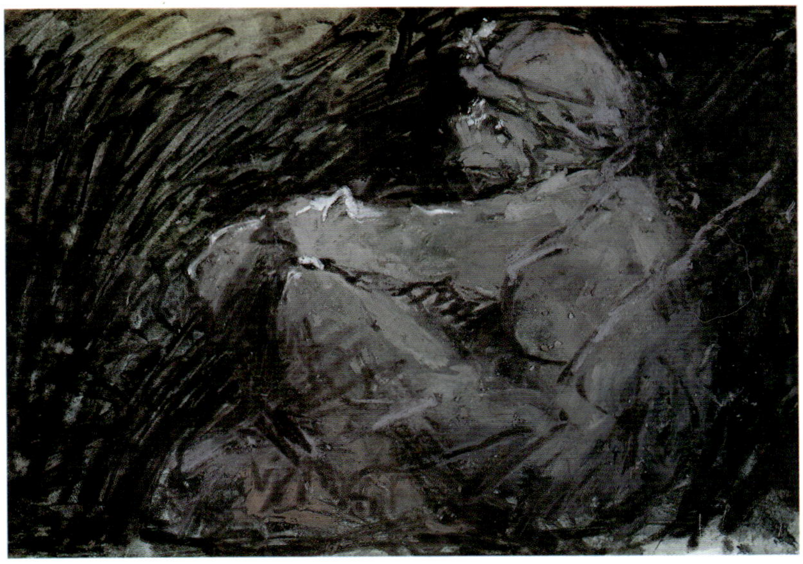

Electricians riding on the conveyor belts November 18th 1983 4.30 p.m. No. 31 panel.

Lower. Miner resting. Oil pastel. Private collection.

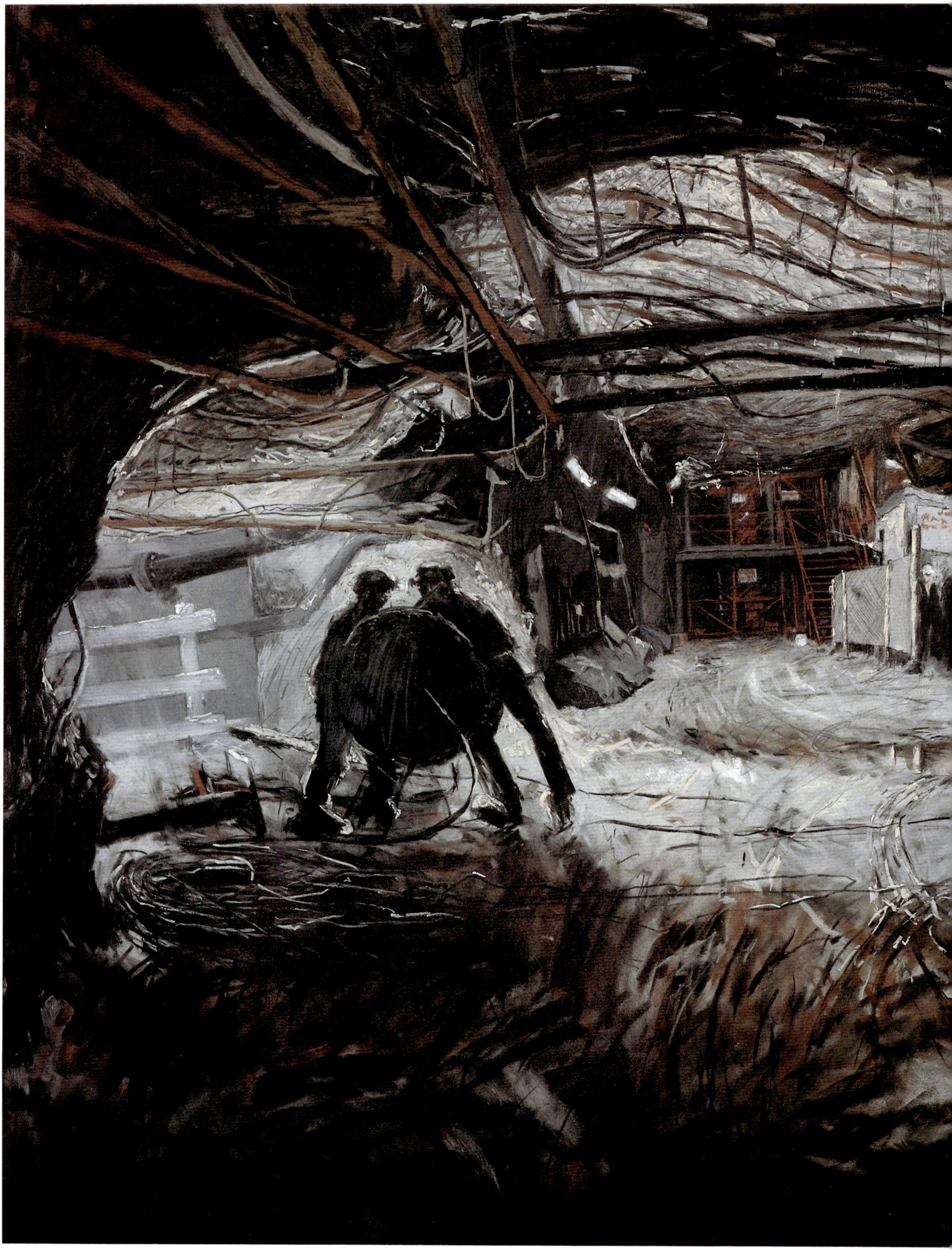

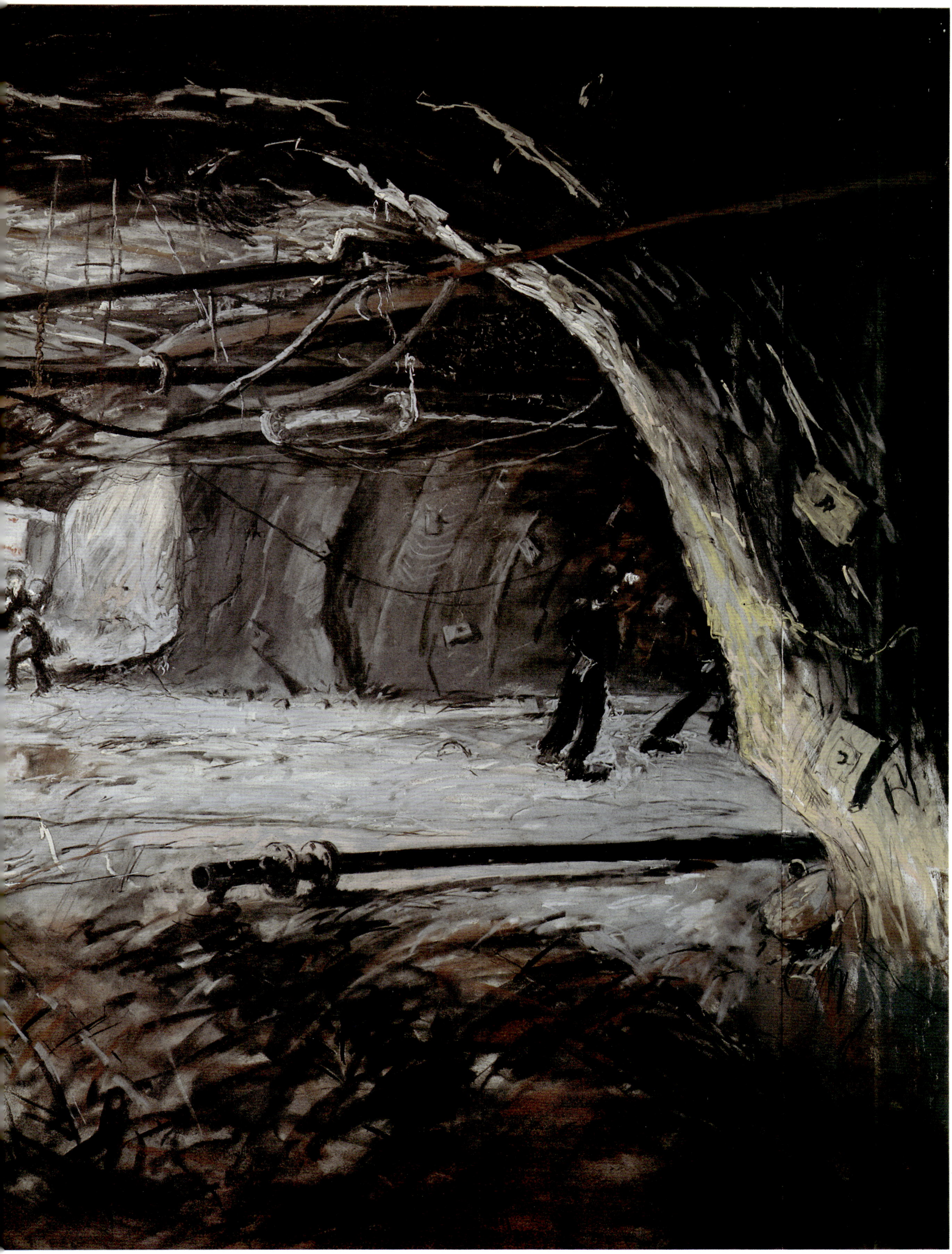

Manshaft, pit bottom, salvage crew stripping out old pipes and cables 1984. Watercolour & charcoal, Conté & Graphite. Private collection.

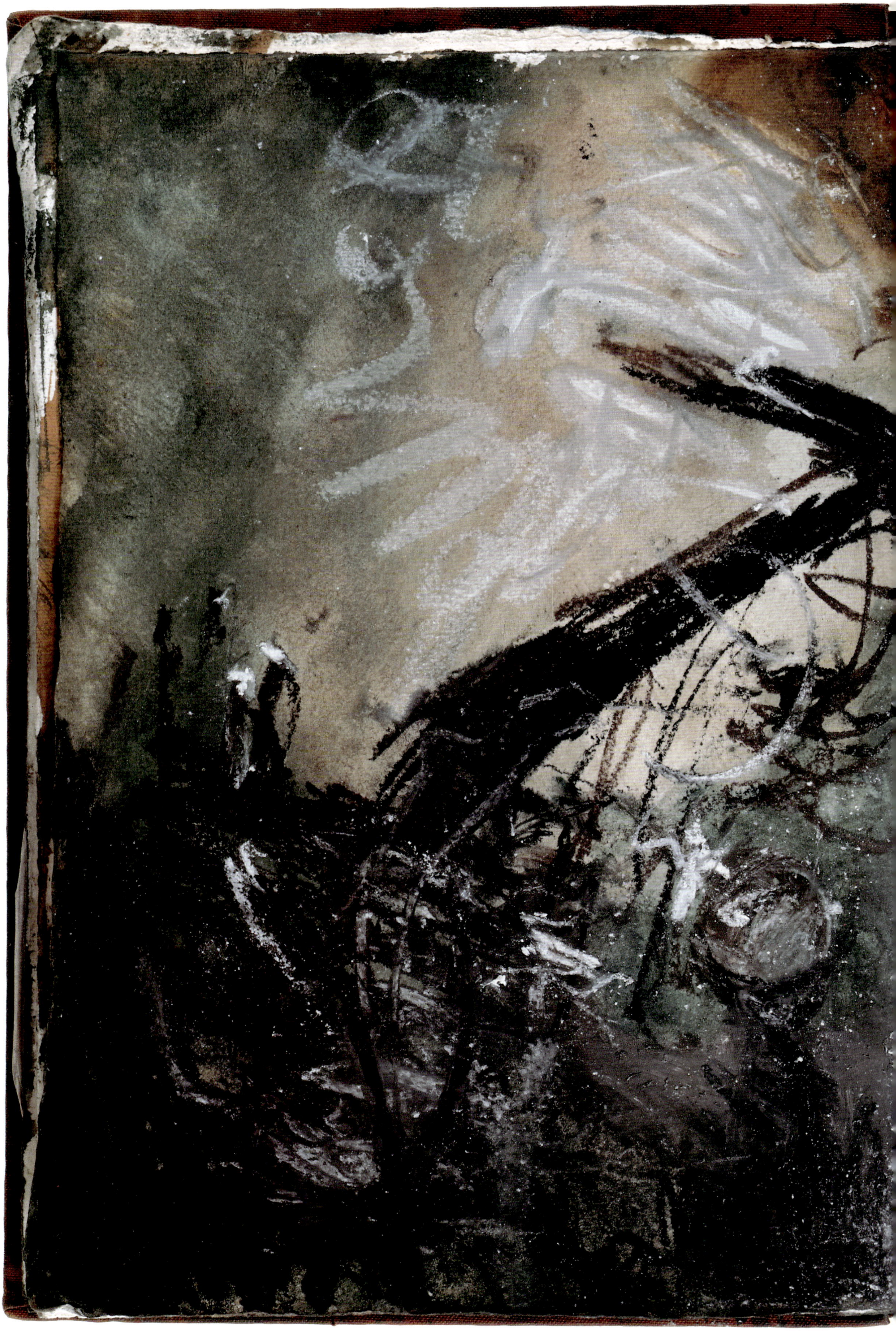

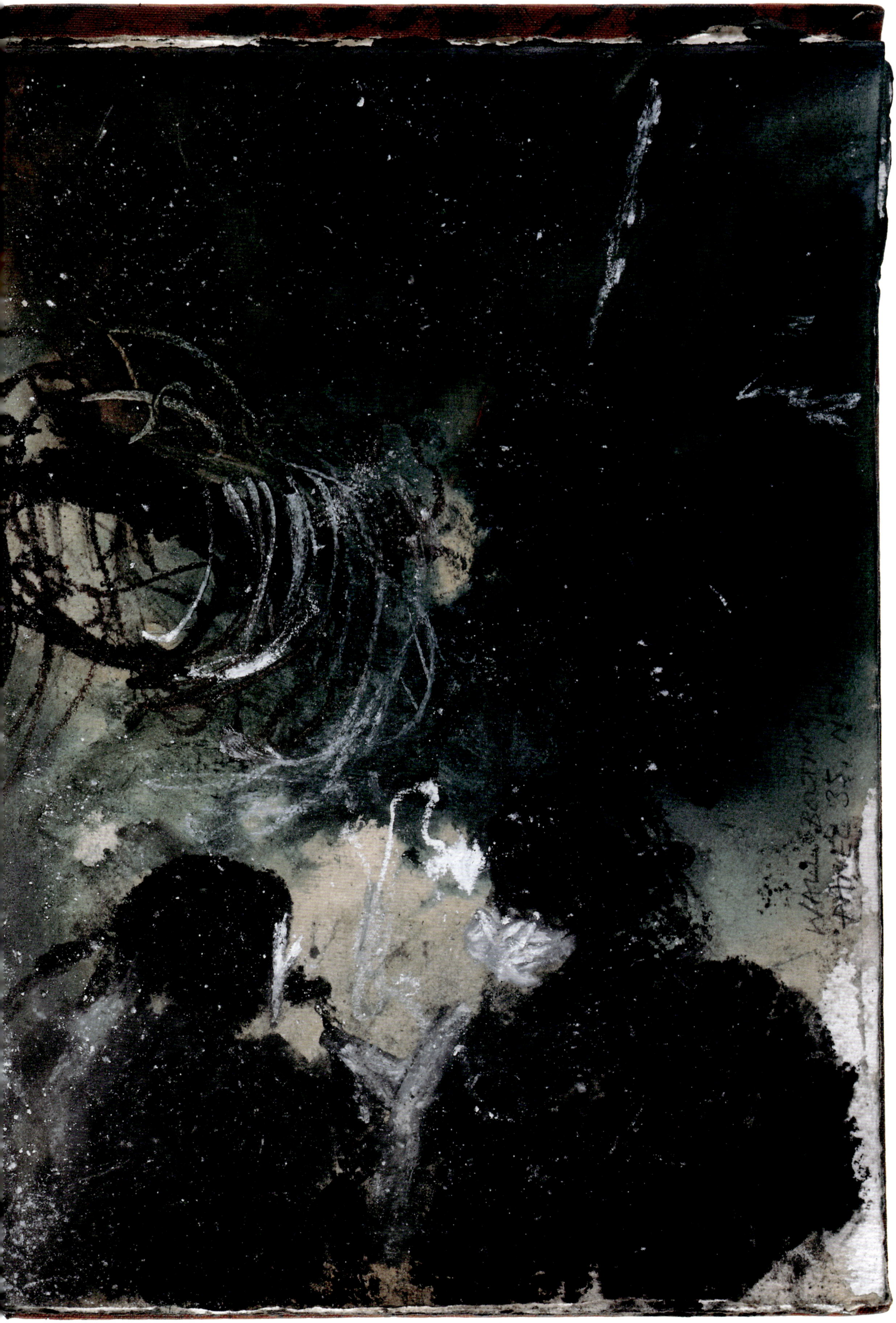

Dennis Hall and his lads wallbolting, panel 35 November 1983. Watercolour in sketchbook. 11¼″×16″.

Conveyor running potash out of No. 31 panel through area of bad roof, well supported by timber packing, worked standing next to the bait 'cabin', November 1983. Charcoal, Graphite & Conté, 22″×30″.

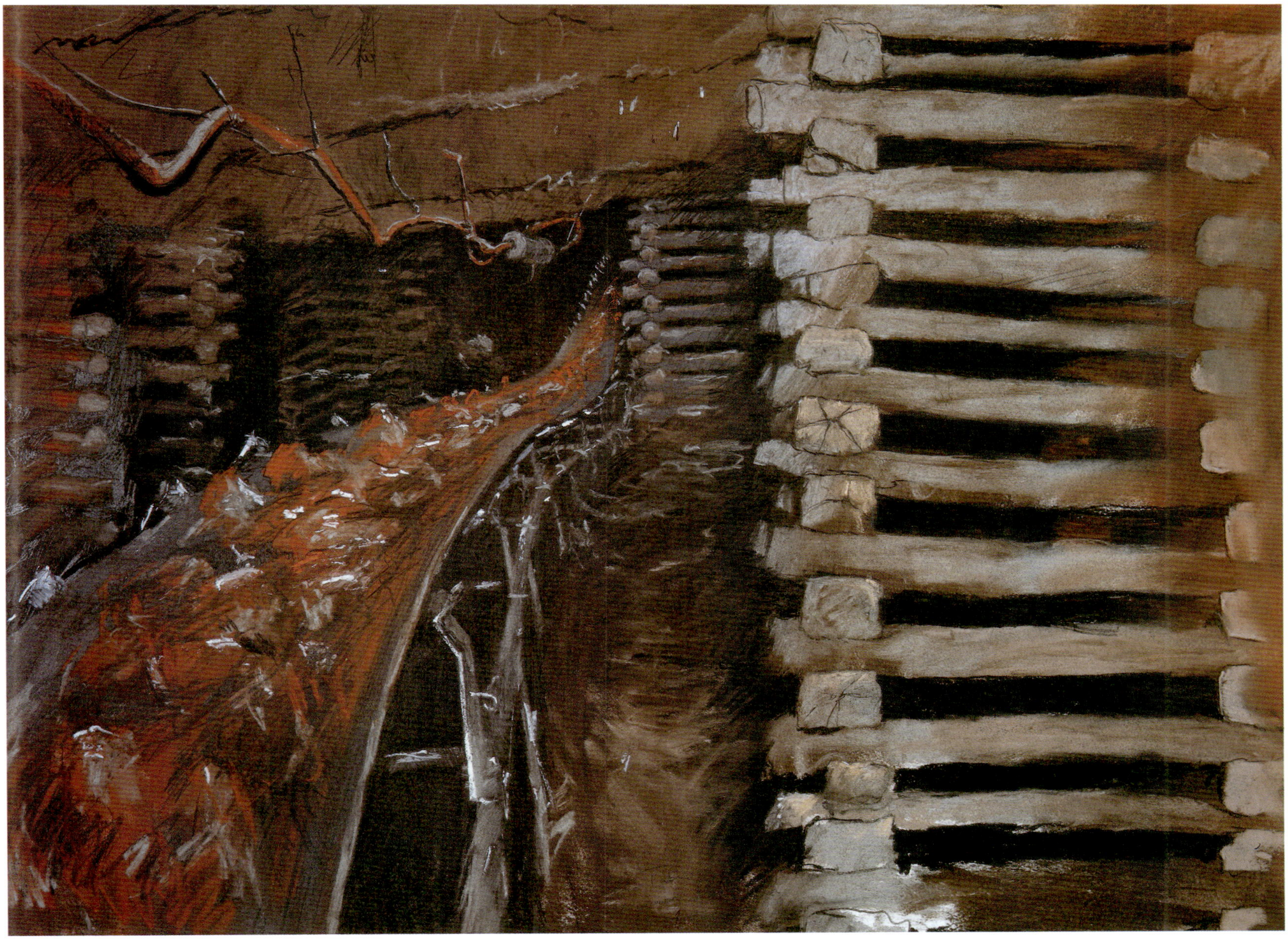

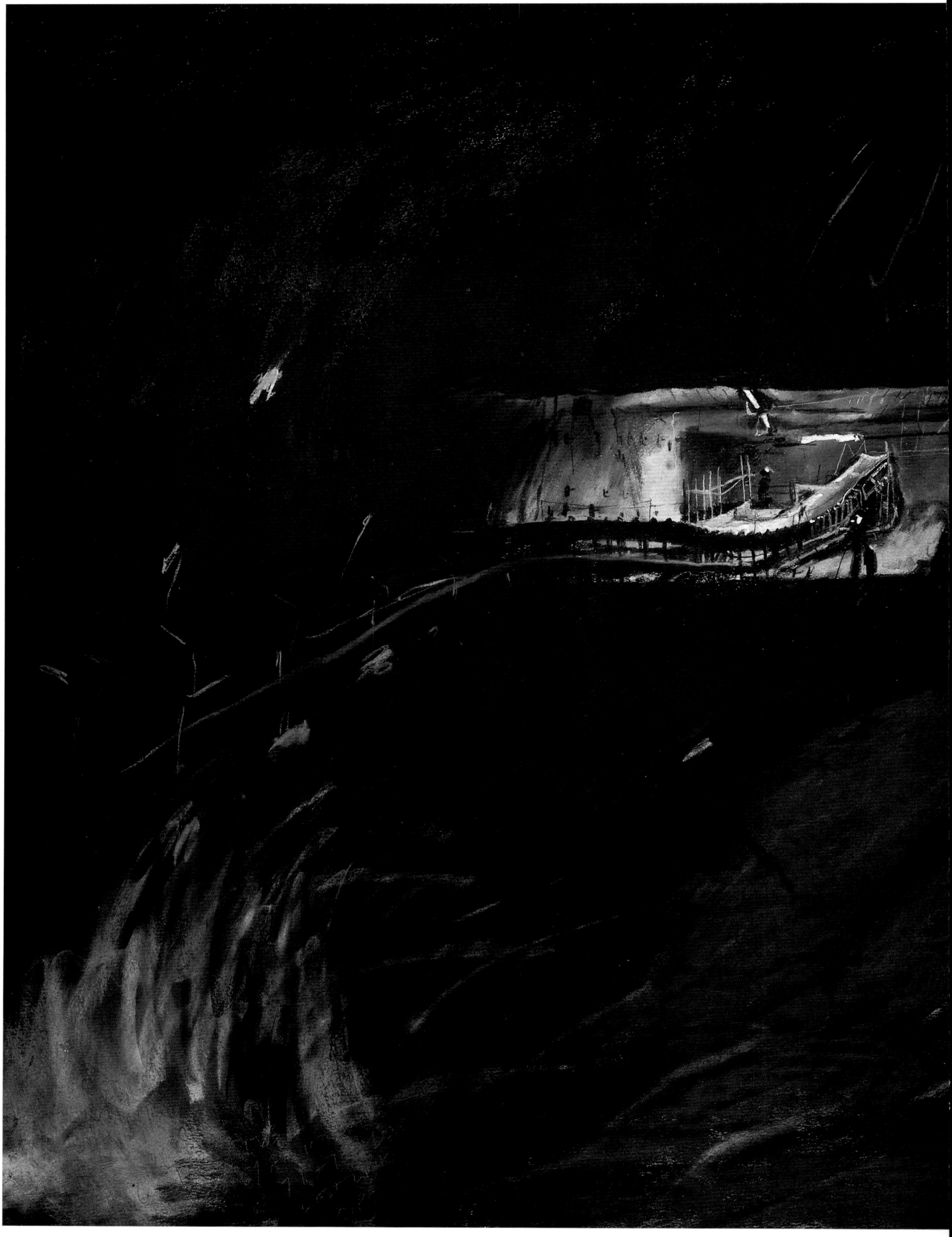

Boarding station at interchange of 7.1 and 7.2 belts, Tommy Lister just coming in for his daily check round. November 1983.
Charcoal & Conté. 31″×53″. Private collection.

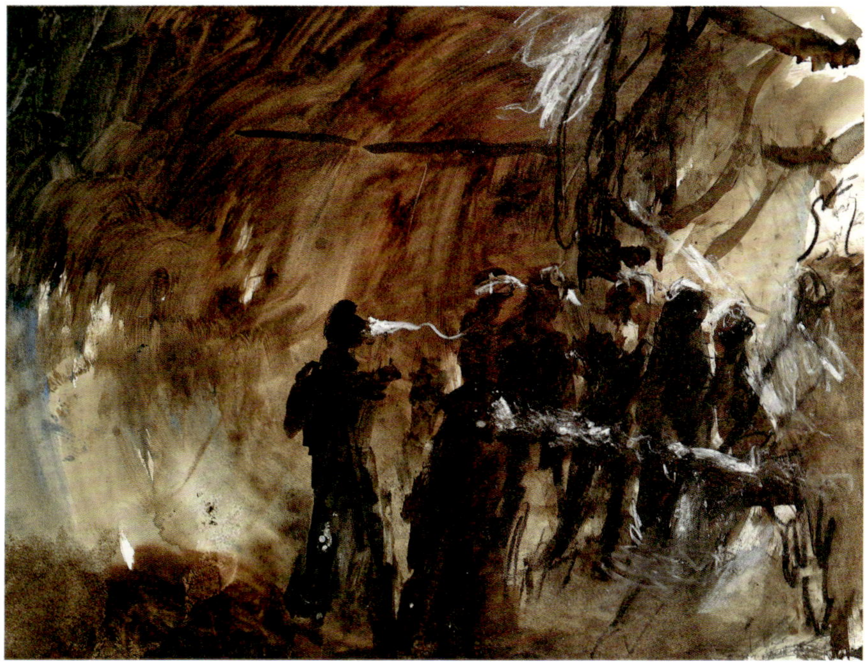

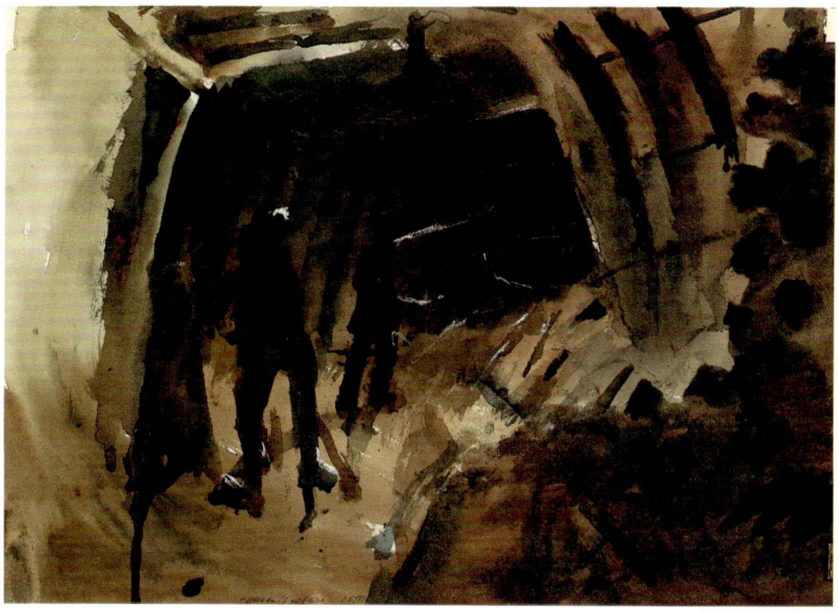

Dennis Hall's lads trying out new air flushing drills panel 29. Watercolour 15″×20″.

Lower. Salvage crew. Watercolour 15″×20″.

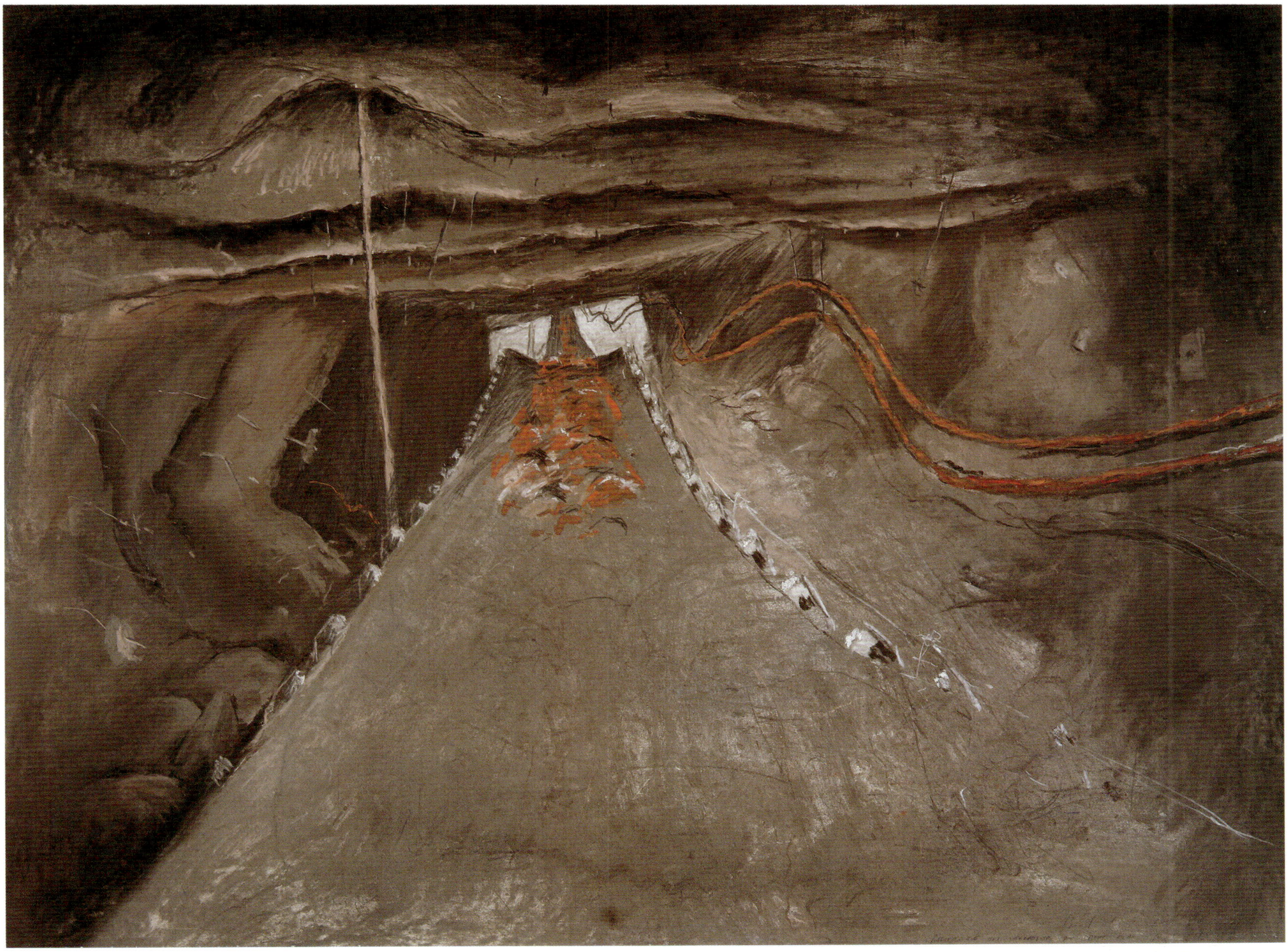

Riding out on the conveyor at the end of the shift. December 24th 1983. Pastel. 30″×40″.

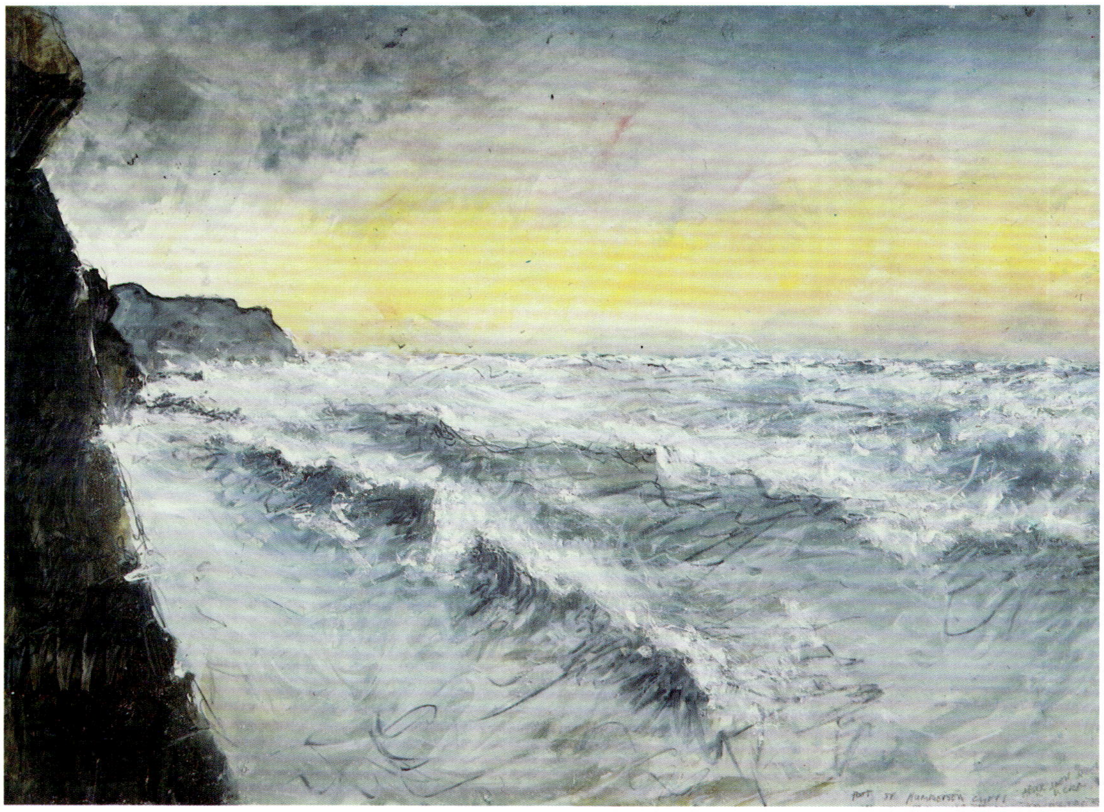

Foot of Hummersea cliffs after snow showers, very cold, 4.00 p.m. 11th November 1985.
Tide just starting to ebb, big surges still running. Watercolour & Graphite. 22″×30″.

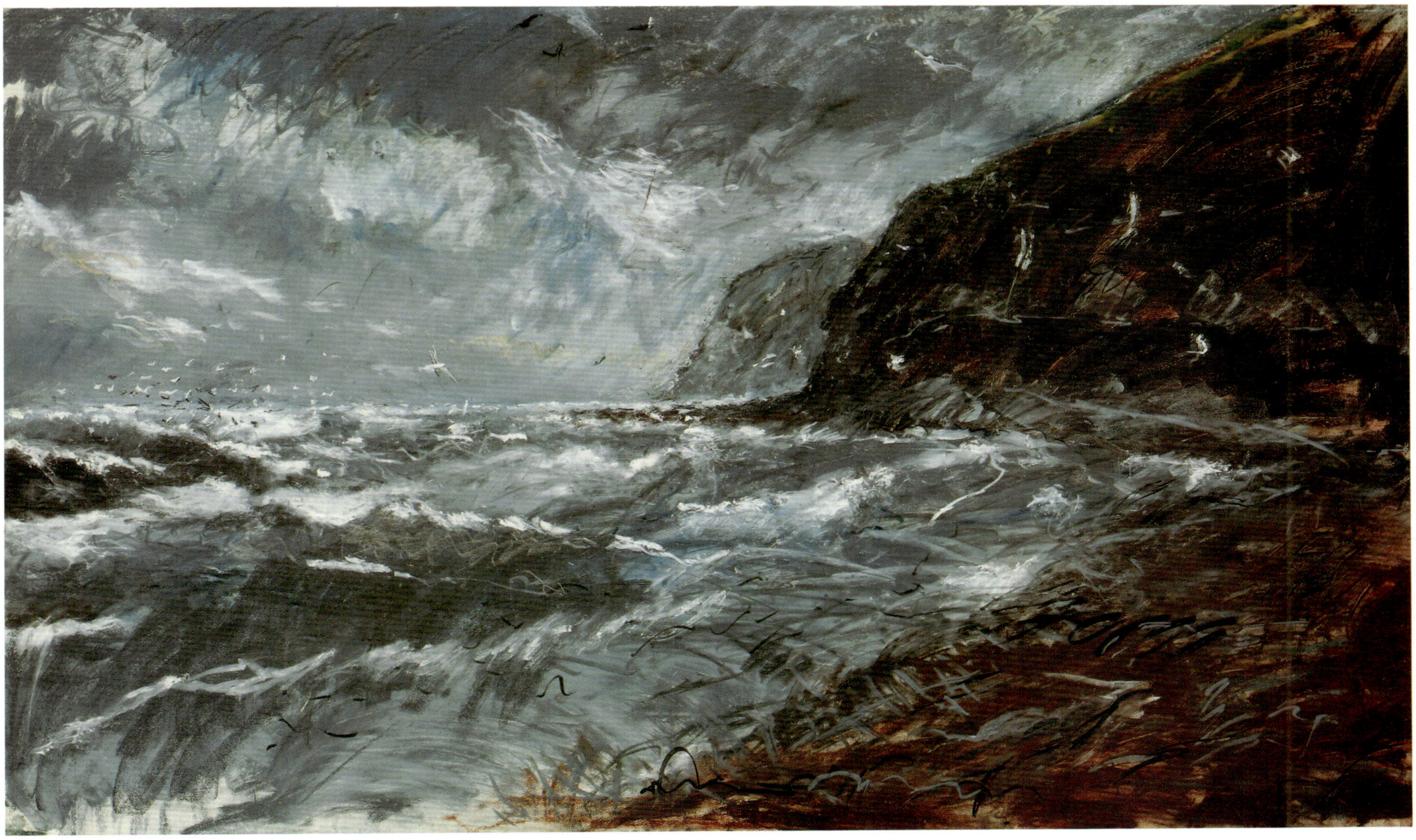

On the foreshore at Skinningrove, wet afternoon, looking along towards Hummersea. Watercolour & Conté. 31″×53″.

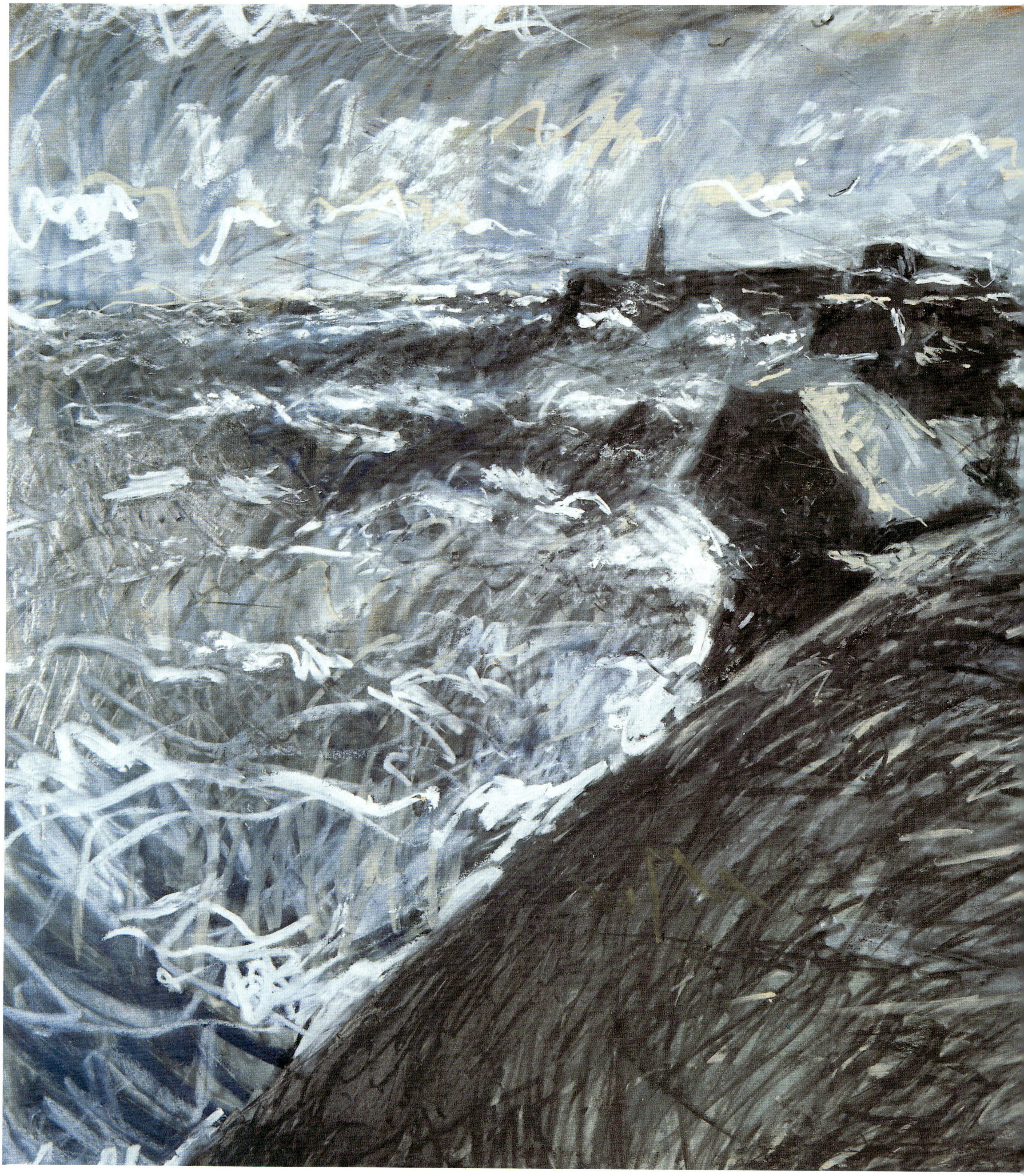

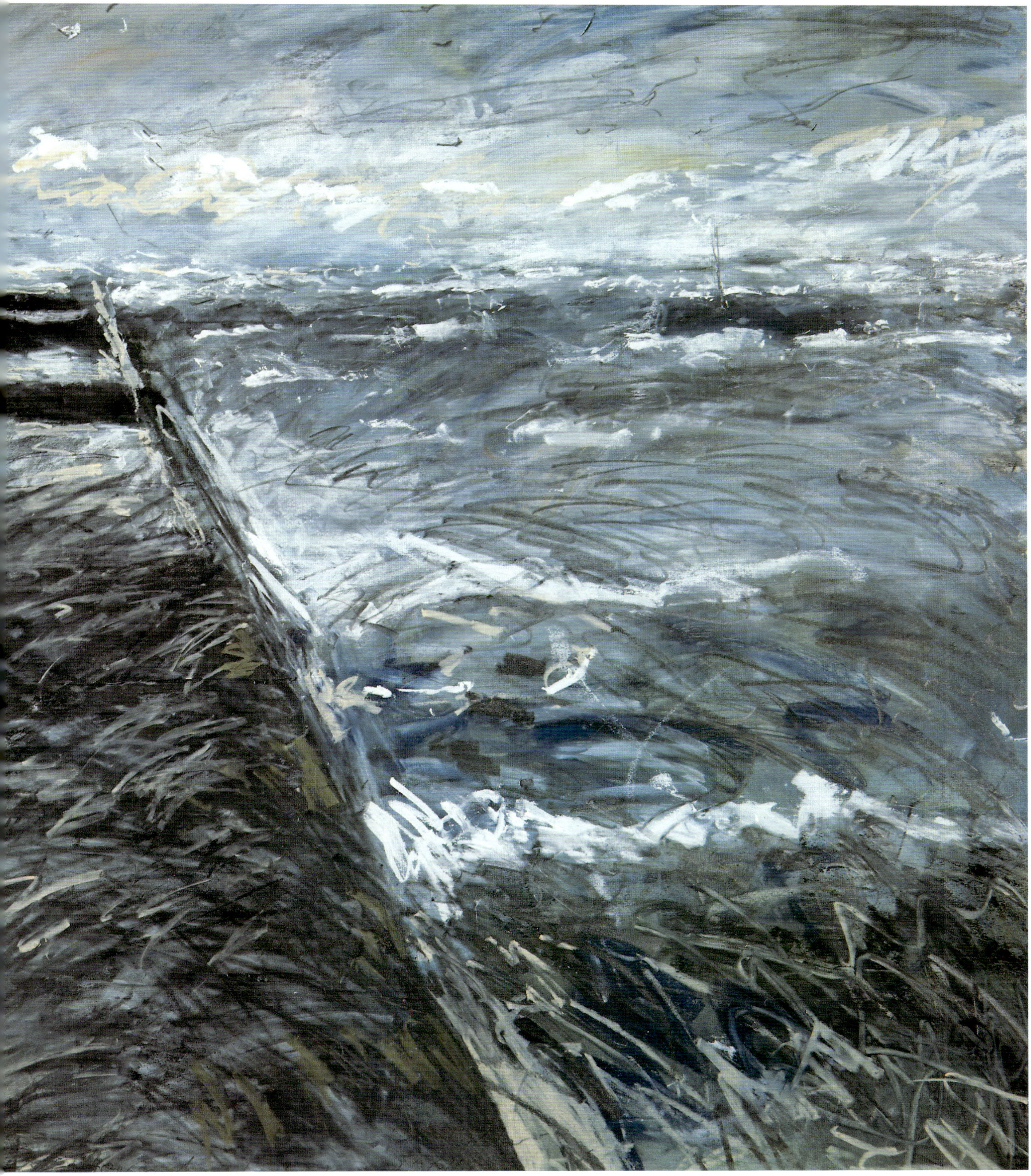

Afternoon December 31st 1980, Cowbar breakwater, tide falling. Watercolour pastel & graphite. 31″×53″.

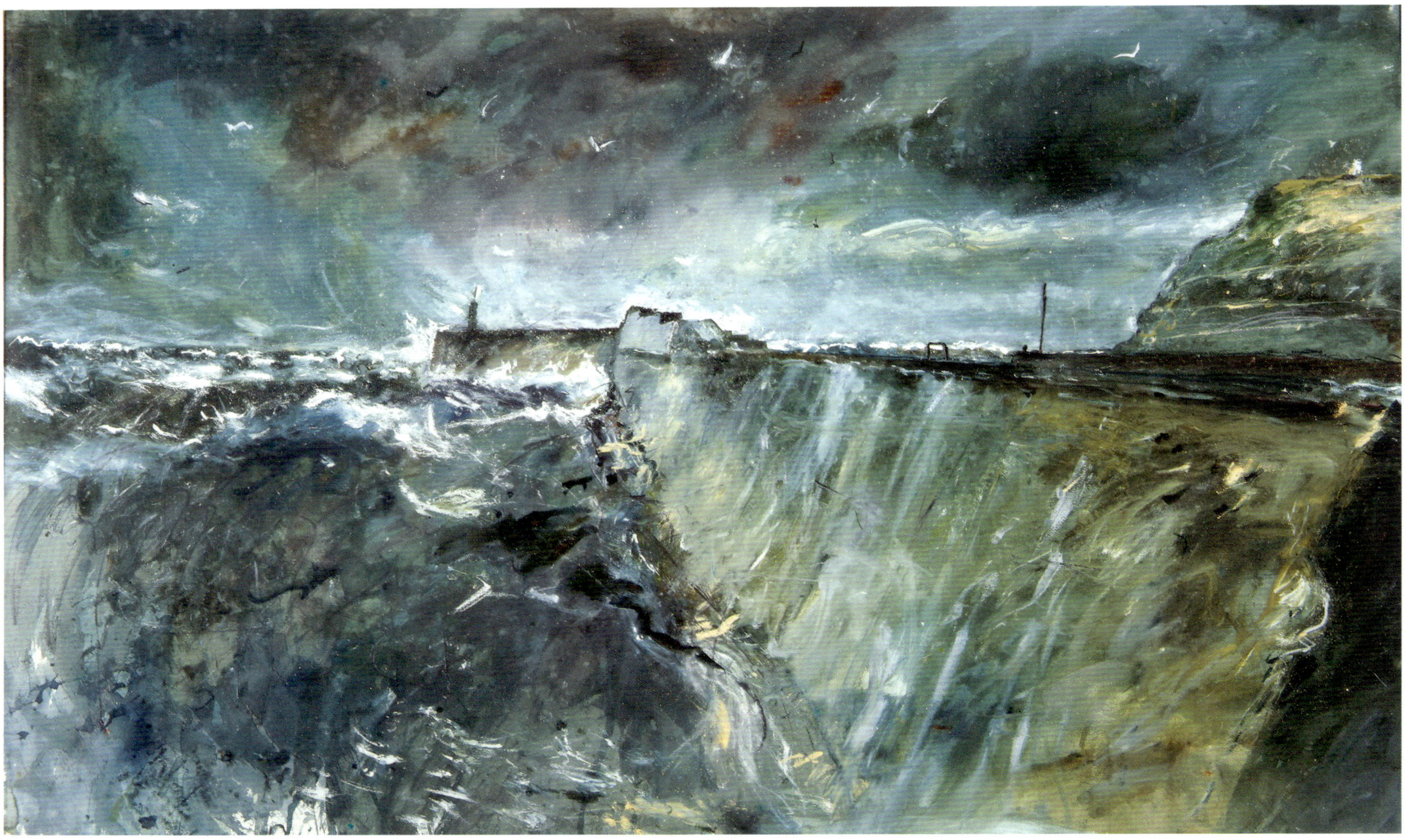

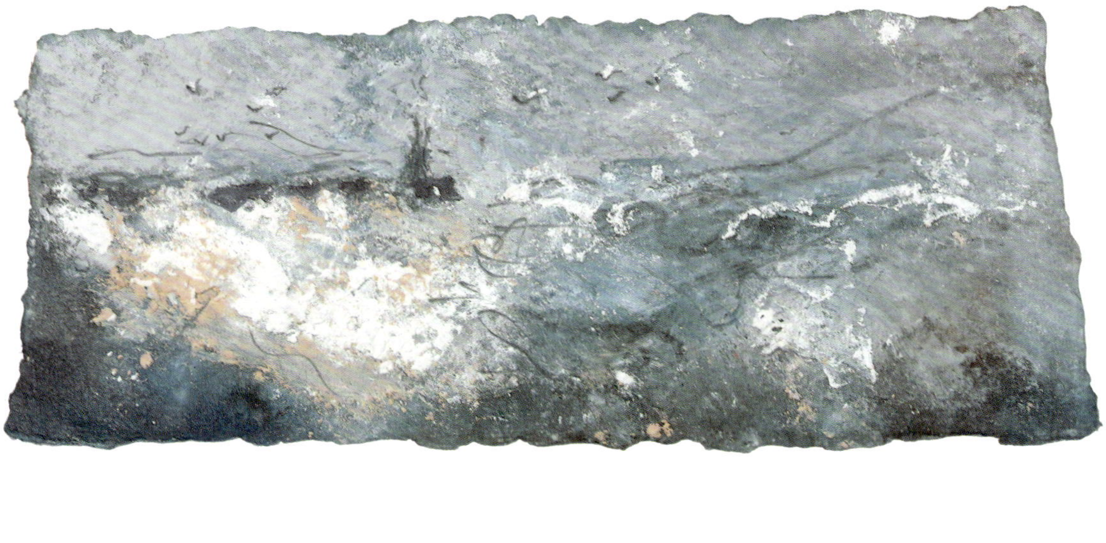

Snow showers all day, Cowbar breakwater, low tide 6–7 p.m. Thursday 24th March 1983. Watercolour. 31″×53″.

Lower. Cowbar breakwater. 1987. Watercolour on fragment of hand made paper, actual size.

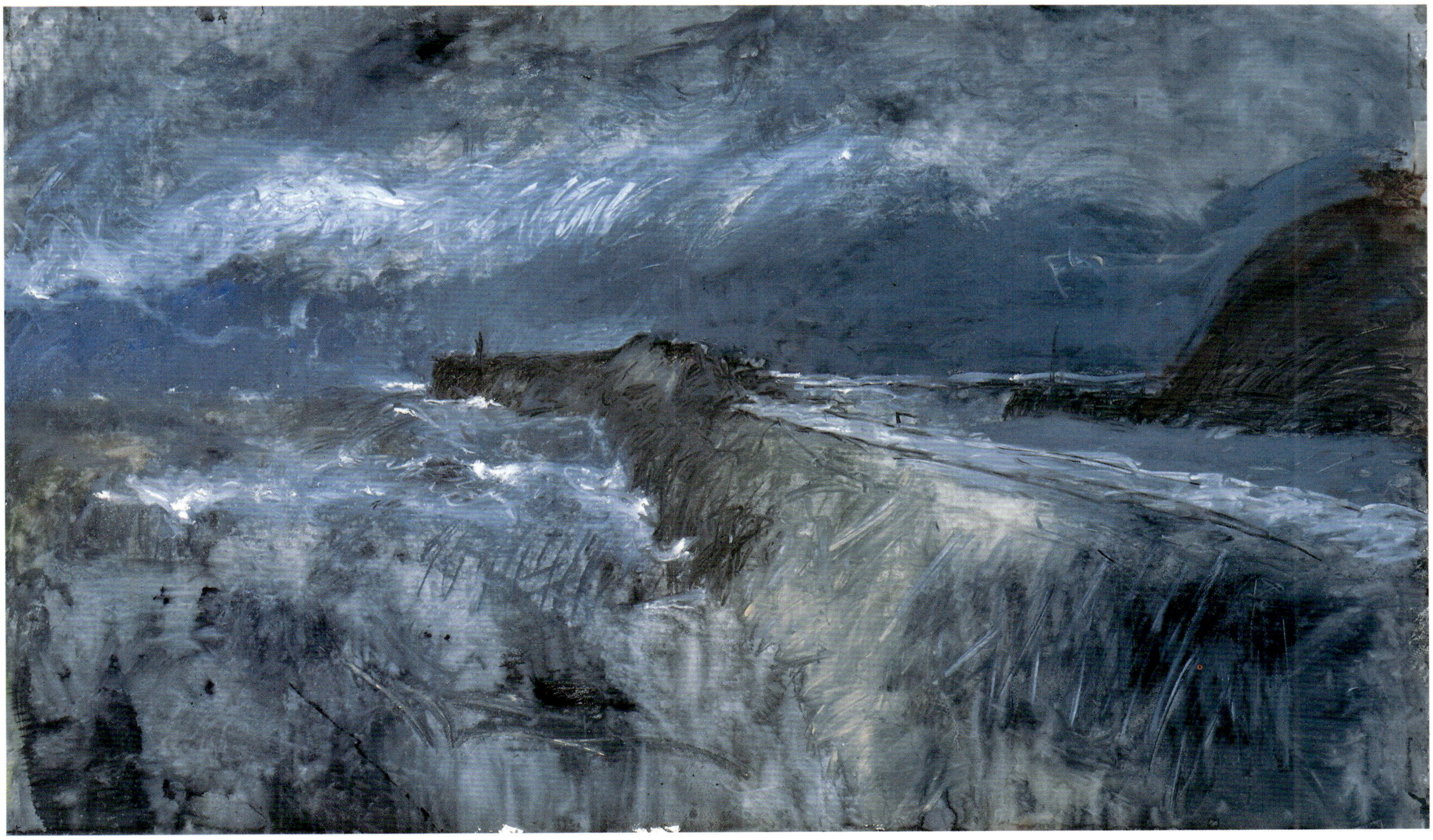

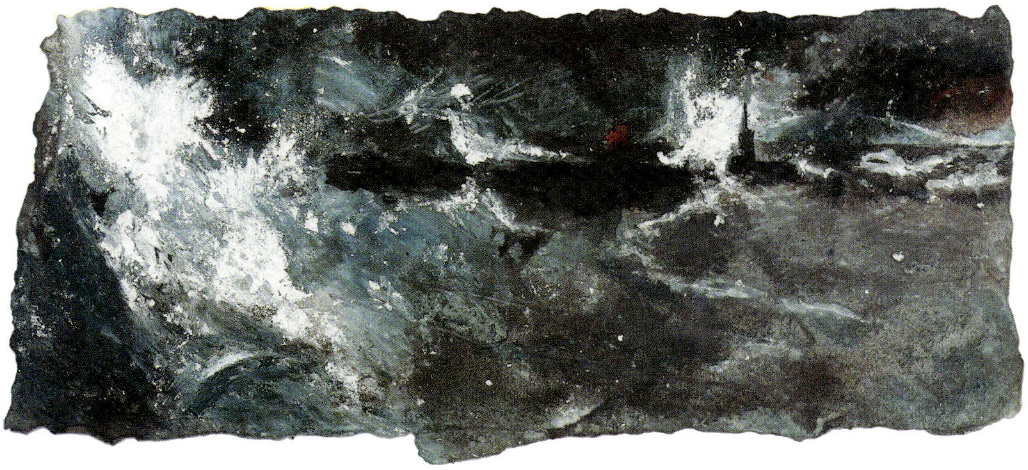

Cowbar breakwater at dusk. December 1988. Watercolour. 31″×53″.

Lower. Moon rising, Cowbar breakwater 1987. Watercolour on fragment of hand made paper, actual size.

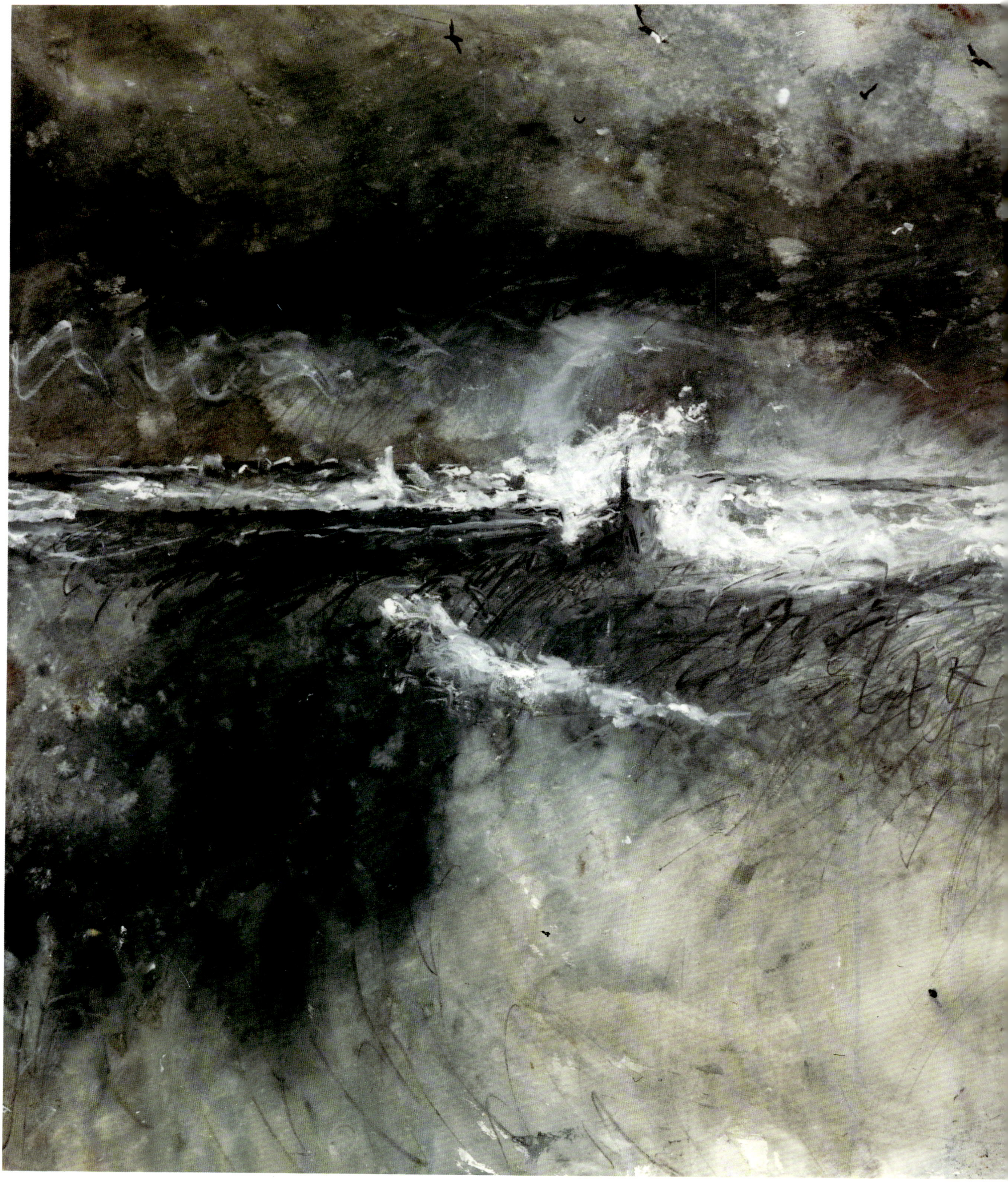

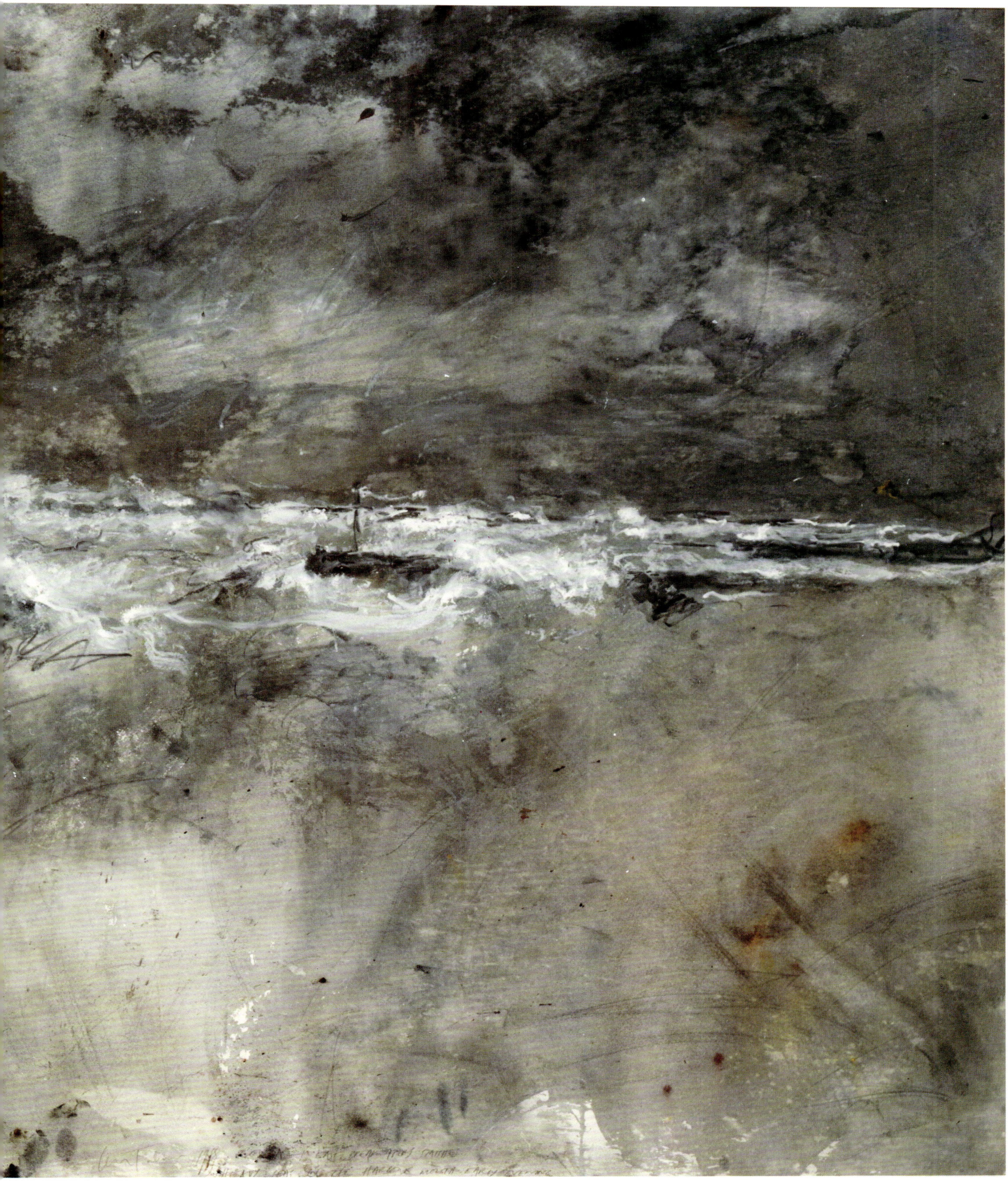

November 1988, heavy seas breaking in Staithes harbour mouth, early evening, North and East breakwaters. Watercolour. 32″×54″.

8.00pm, September 18th, 1985. Arrive South Gare – raining steadily and already almost dark – except that the whole world seems to be lit up by flare stacks and blast furnace floodlighting. Lots of water on the road and steam riotous in an orange sky. Get soaked – for the second time tonight – carrying gear down to cabin. No sign of Ian. Shutters down and put the kettle on. Sitting in the quiet by the window, a whole string of orange lights across in Durham. Kettle to the boil for a pot of tea. Sat there with a wax candle on the table and the paraffin lamp over the sink turned low. The rain still steady outside. Wonder if there is any chance of working – feel more like going to sleep. Tea's made – make a full pot in case Ian gets down, but drink only half of it. Green lights flashing in the river towards Seaton Power Station. Curlew and small waders calling, sitting an hour when banging outside gets me up to investigate but only two lads putting gear into a dingy ready to make an early start tomorrow. Anyway I'm up out of the chair so pick up gear, lock cabin and walk down round the back of cabin and along to the pilot jetty – still raining steadily but not too hard and no wind – both river and sea like a mill pond. Pilot jetty railings just been repaired and repainted – white against the black night and the wet paint spattered walkway. Down by the cutter for half an hour watching the night – watching the beautiful functional form of the boat rocking at her berth, watching the rain on the flat calm river, listening to the lap of water and the raucous chatter of Tees Harbour Radio coming up from the wheelhouse. The odd grey form gliding through the blackness of the night. Resting now on new white railings making a study of the darkness of the river mouth – the mystery beyond the lights – the depths and distant awayness of the dark, inky night sea, where I cannot see but only feel for the space which eludes me in the darkness.

Later, sitting on the concrete breakwater top with a drawing board on edge as a seat – still raining – drawing or painting – I don't know which, looking along to Coatham from this higher viewpoint – sands rising beneath me almost orange but grey, the lights of Redcar and the sea reaching to the dunes. Row of orange yellow points of light at Coatham the darkness of the dunes rising and undulating and away to the right crazy, amazing floodlighting casting a weird glow over sand, sea and sky. The rain taking more of my drawing or watercolour away than I can get down. I eventually close up the book and wander along the beach – loose, frothed up, new blown sand, higher massed up than it has been – traces of seacoal – but no supplies for my winter fire. Wander over the dunes and am set upon by two barking dogs, lampglows from a couple of cabins and pass a word or two with an old man figure smelling slightly beery in the dark. Over the top and deposit drawings into the cabin to dry. Rain eased off and still no wind, so carry dingy down to the water's edge, oars, a new bag of bits and a drawing board. Everything so still and silent and beautiful as the boat glides effortlessly through the still water – unlike Saturday when I had to struggle to row 40 yards to the coble. Now past the coble the wall end and out into the river itself where I row out towards mid stream, behind me, not two miles distant the throb and roar of Redcar blast furnace like a vast flat illuminated freize against the sky. A photographers paradise with its immense silhouetted forms wrapped in steam and violent reflections. But on still, at my back on the boats heading, lies the dark silent sea a vast blackness.

Way out into the river, I drift on the tide, small sprats leaping out of the water close to the oars. Eventually pick up a small mooring dan and hitch the painter to it so that I swing to the tide head up stream but me facing the darkness of the sea, rocking silently. Set up my board and paint for an hour or so till lack of light and the onset of more rain forces a stop and have to cover my board and row for the hole to stop too much watercolour being washed away. Curlew calling as I worked and silent grey gulls gliding through my mysterious blackness. A whole string of lights to Hartlepool. Yellow again, bar a red and green to mark the channel – to seaward a strong red and a string of three progressively distant greens flash and wink towards the fairway. To the right the white beam of the lighthouse stretches into the night. Rowing steadily back into the hole and carry gear up to the cabin where I light the tilley lamp and then carry up the dingy and moor for the night by the 'Veronique'. A pan of of hot milk and a pot of cocoa while I write and go through the night's gleanings – now 2.00am – time to turn into bed. Curlew still call as they drop down onto the mud to feed. A window rattles in the gentle breeze. Green lights still flash out in the channel and the lamp's hiss grows soft.

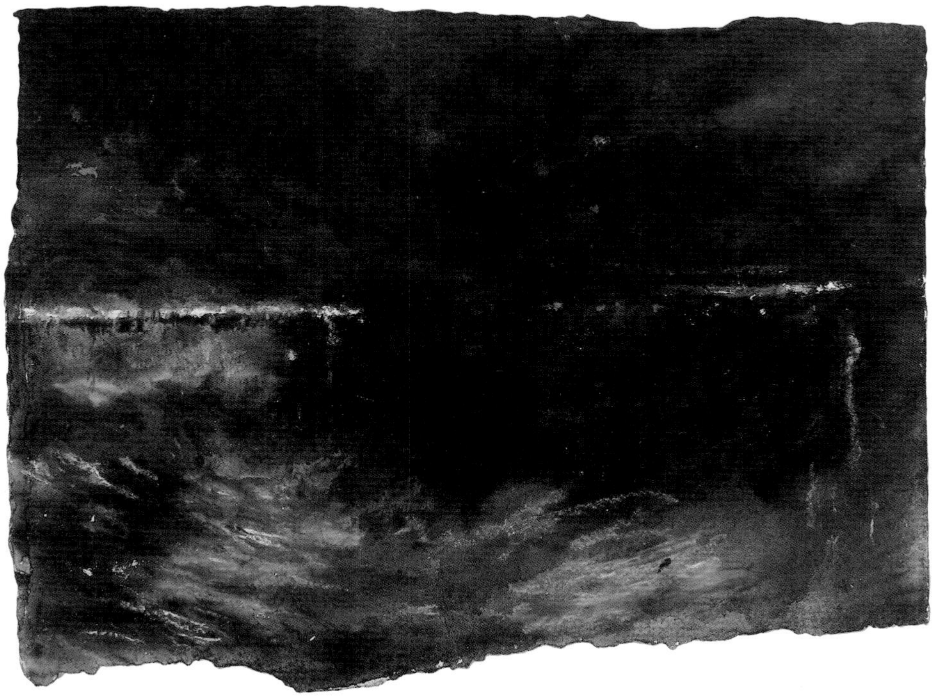

River Tees, looking out to sea, 1.0 a.m. September 19th 1985. Watercolour. 12″×15¾″.

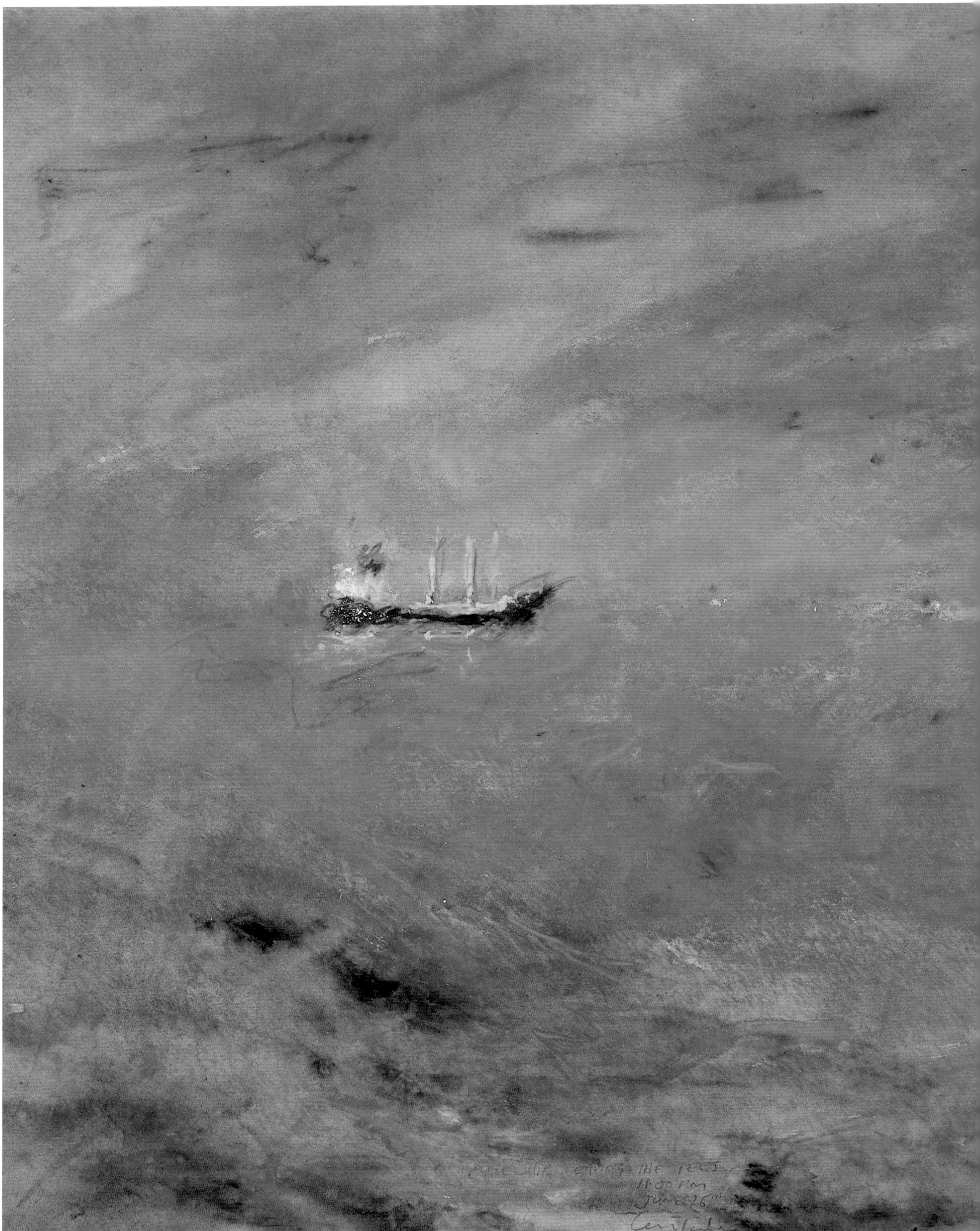
THE TEES
11.00 PM
JUNE 26TH

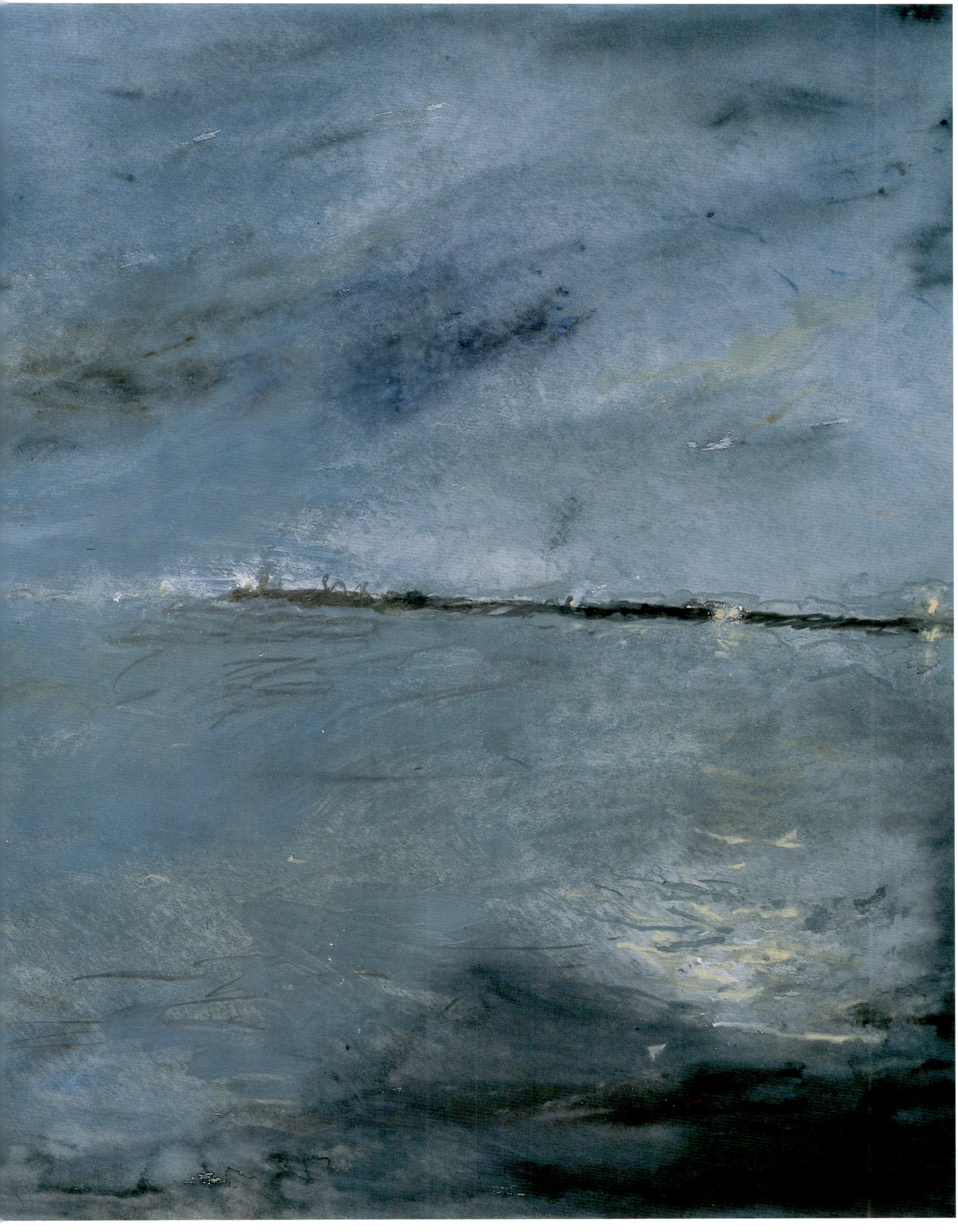

Small ship leaving the Tees 11.00 p.m. June 26th 1989. Raining solidly. Watercolour. 31″×53″.

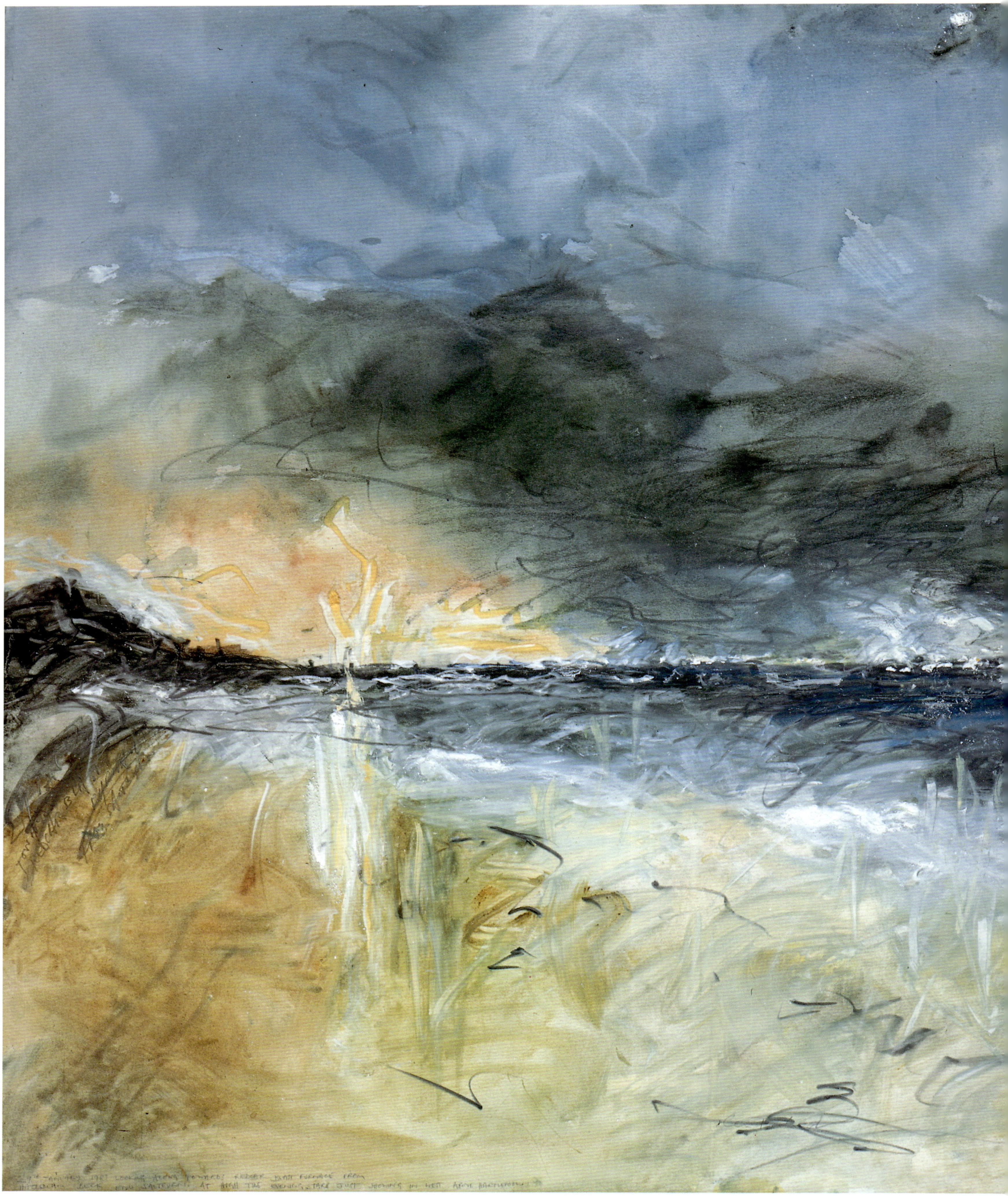

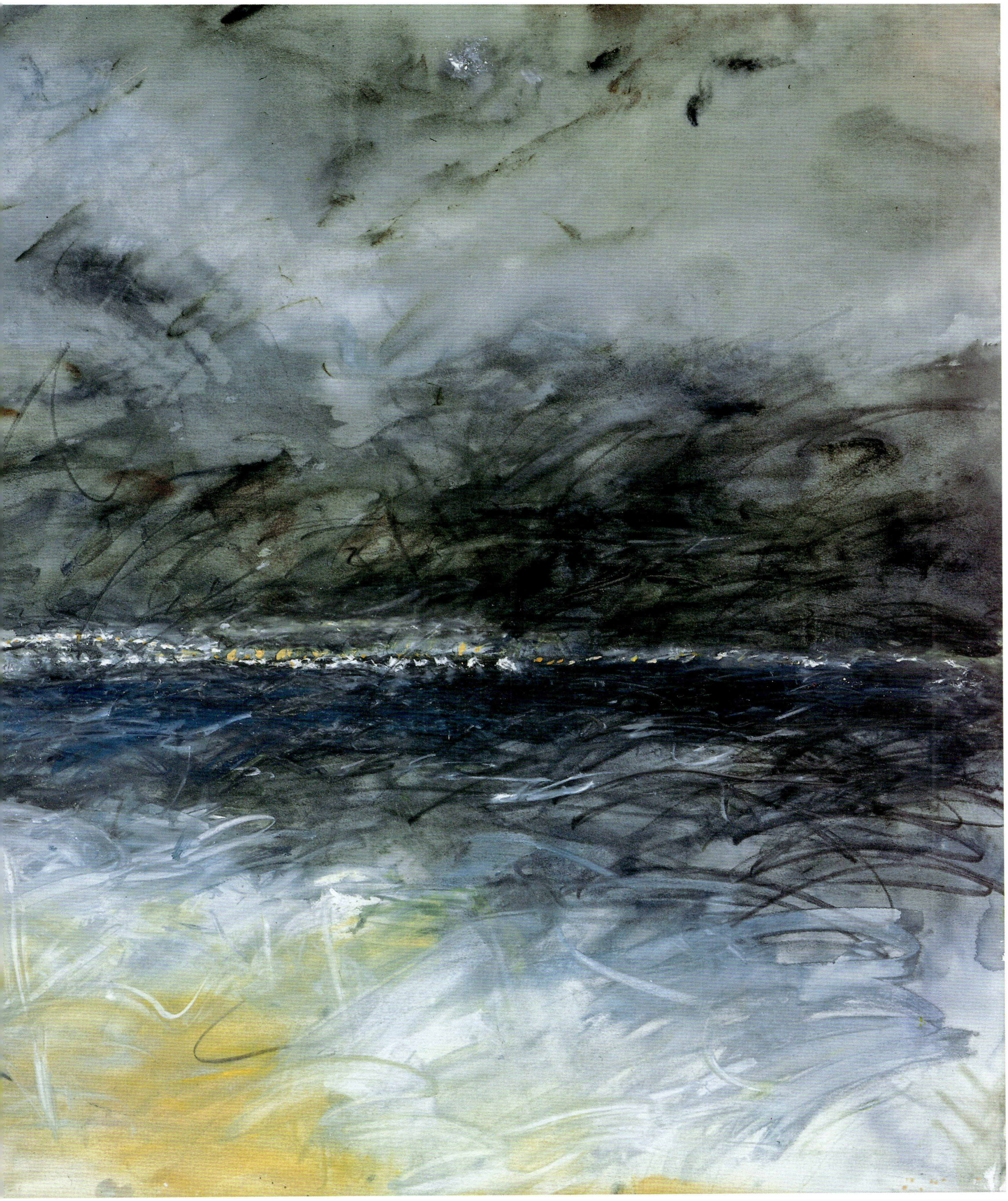

29th January 1983, looking along towards Redcar blast furnace from Hazelgrove beck end Saltburn at high tide. Evening stars just showing in the west above Hartlepool. Watercolour. 31″×53″.

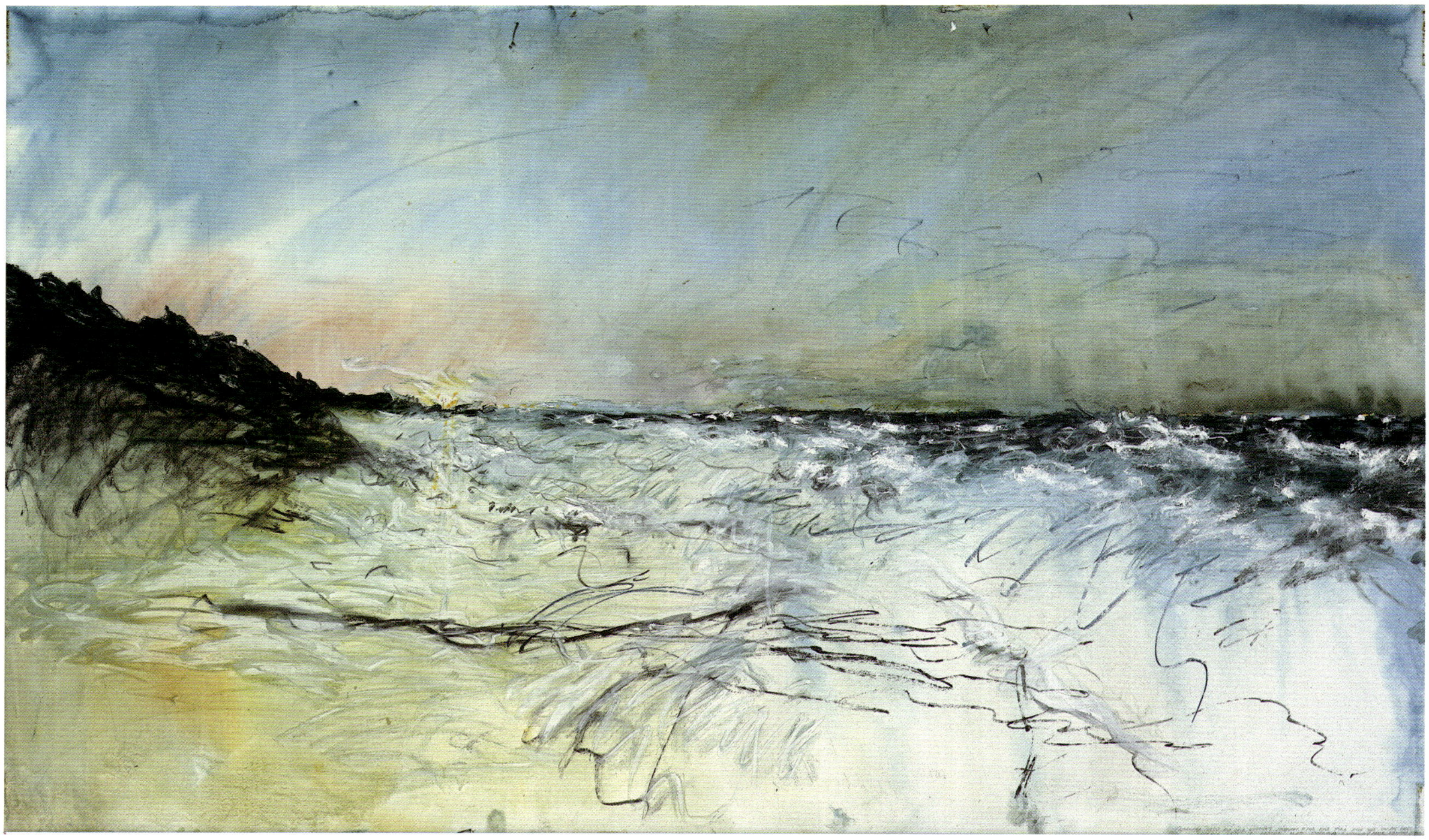

Hard driving seas Saltburn, January 1983, high tide, extremely cold. Watercolour 31″×53″ private collection.

Man running with a dog on Coatham sands. I. Watercolour on fragment of hand made paper 7½″×11¼″. Private collection.

Lower. Man with a dog on Coatham sands III Watercolour on fragment of hand made paper 7½″×11½″ Private collection.

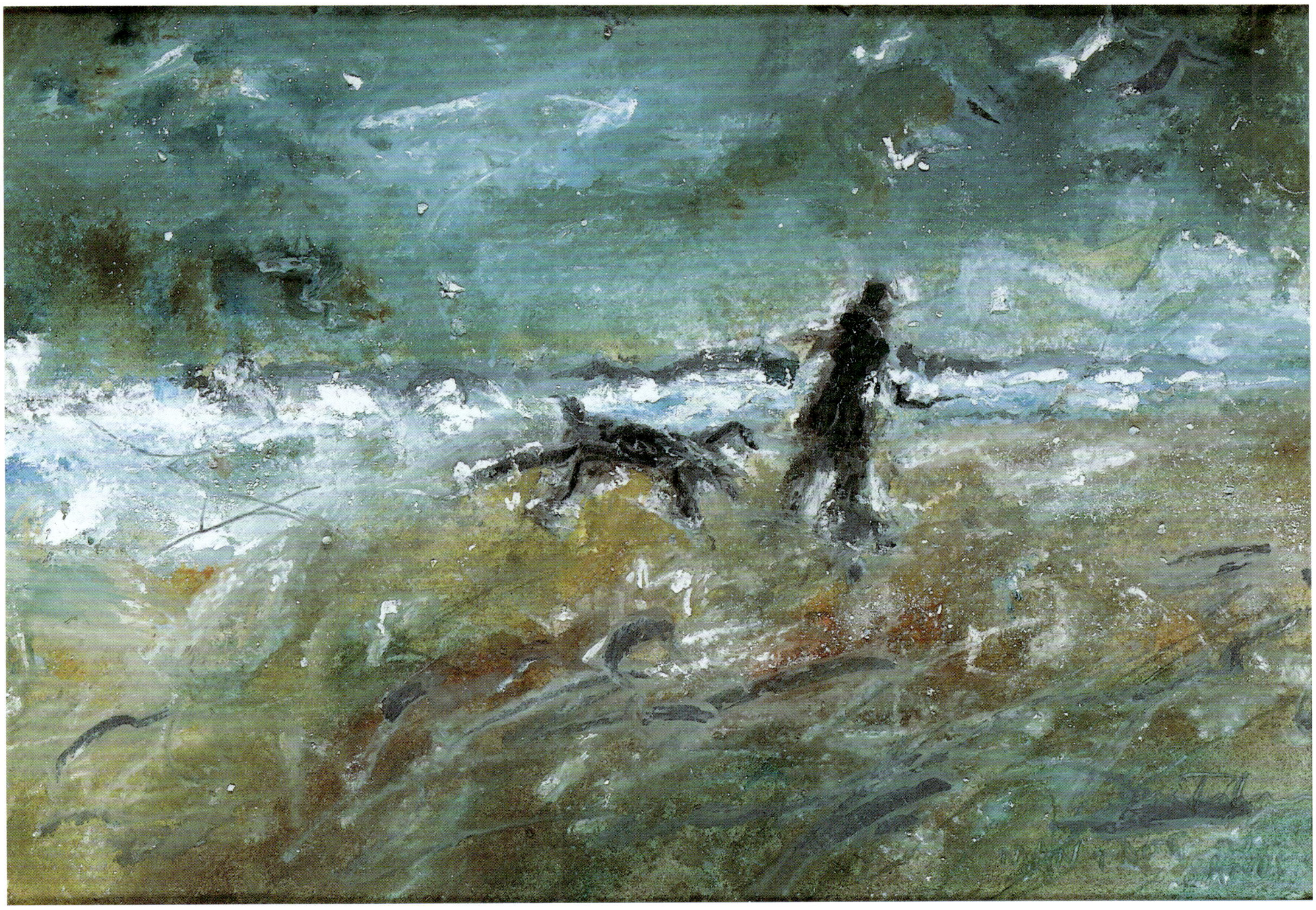

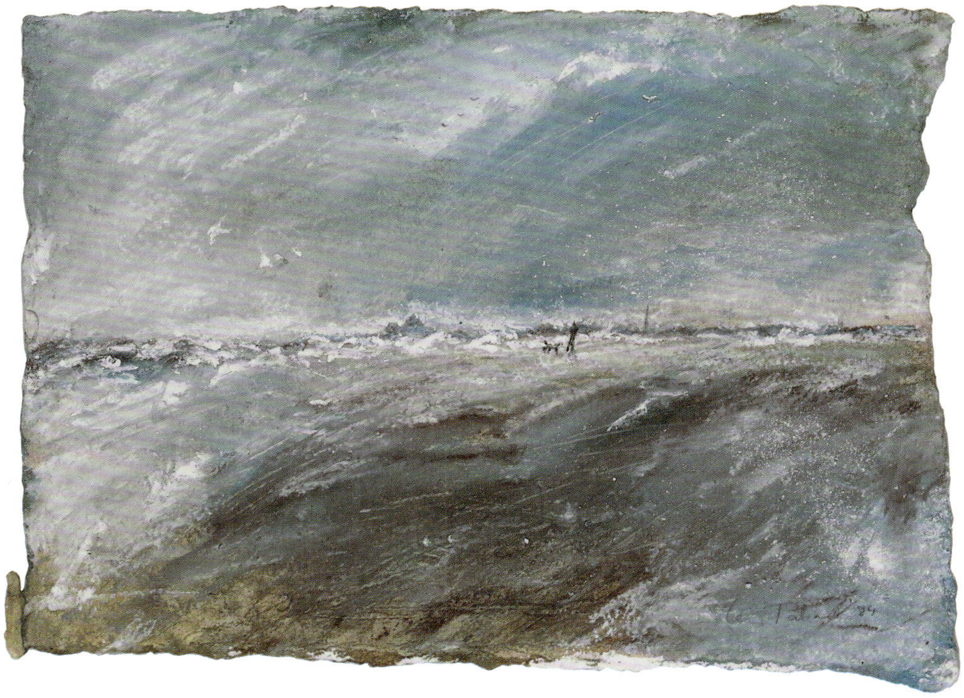

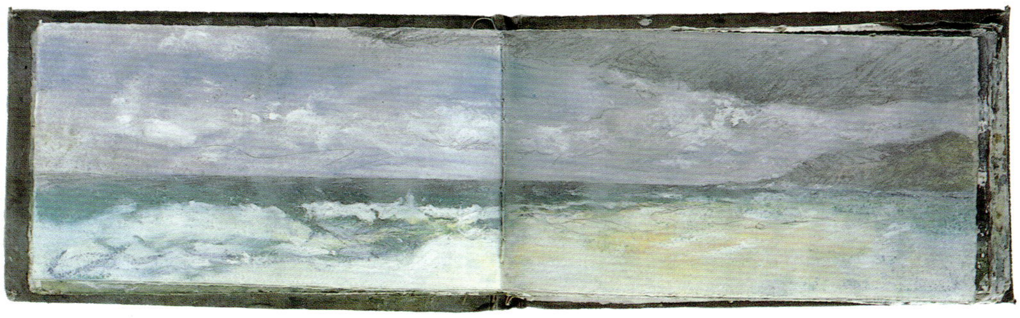

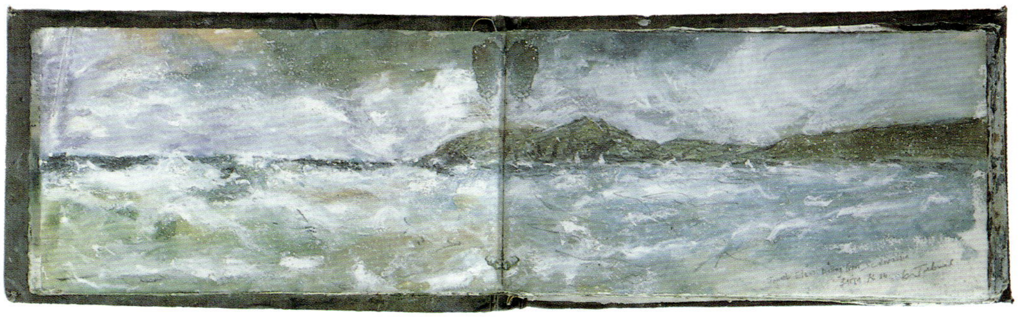

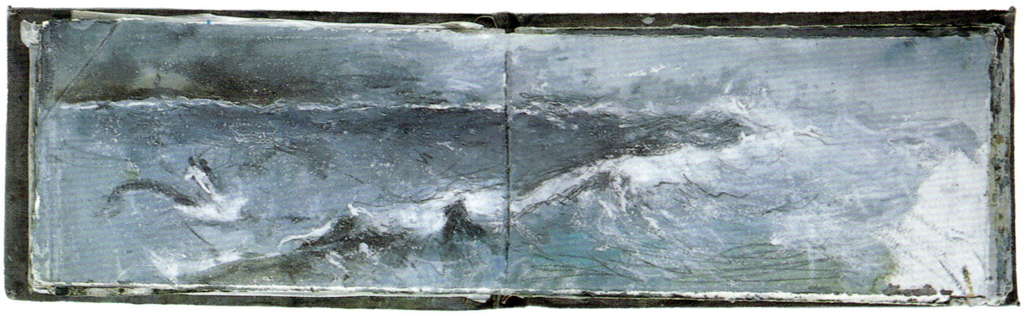

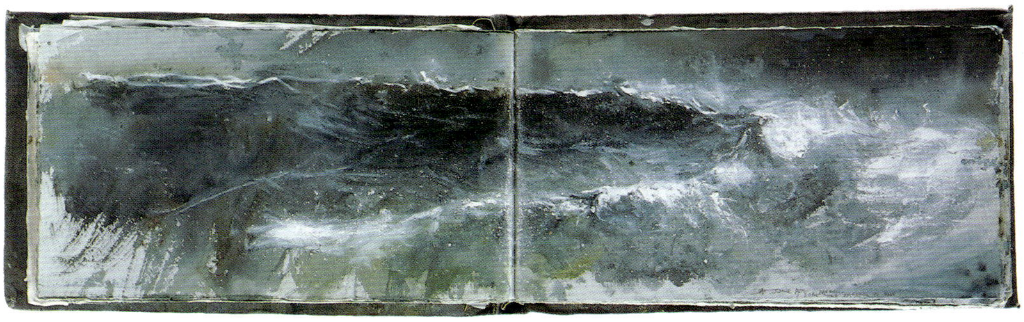

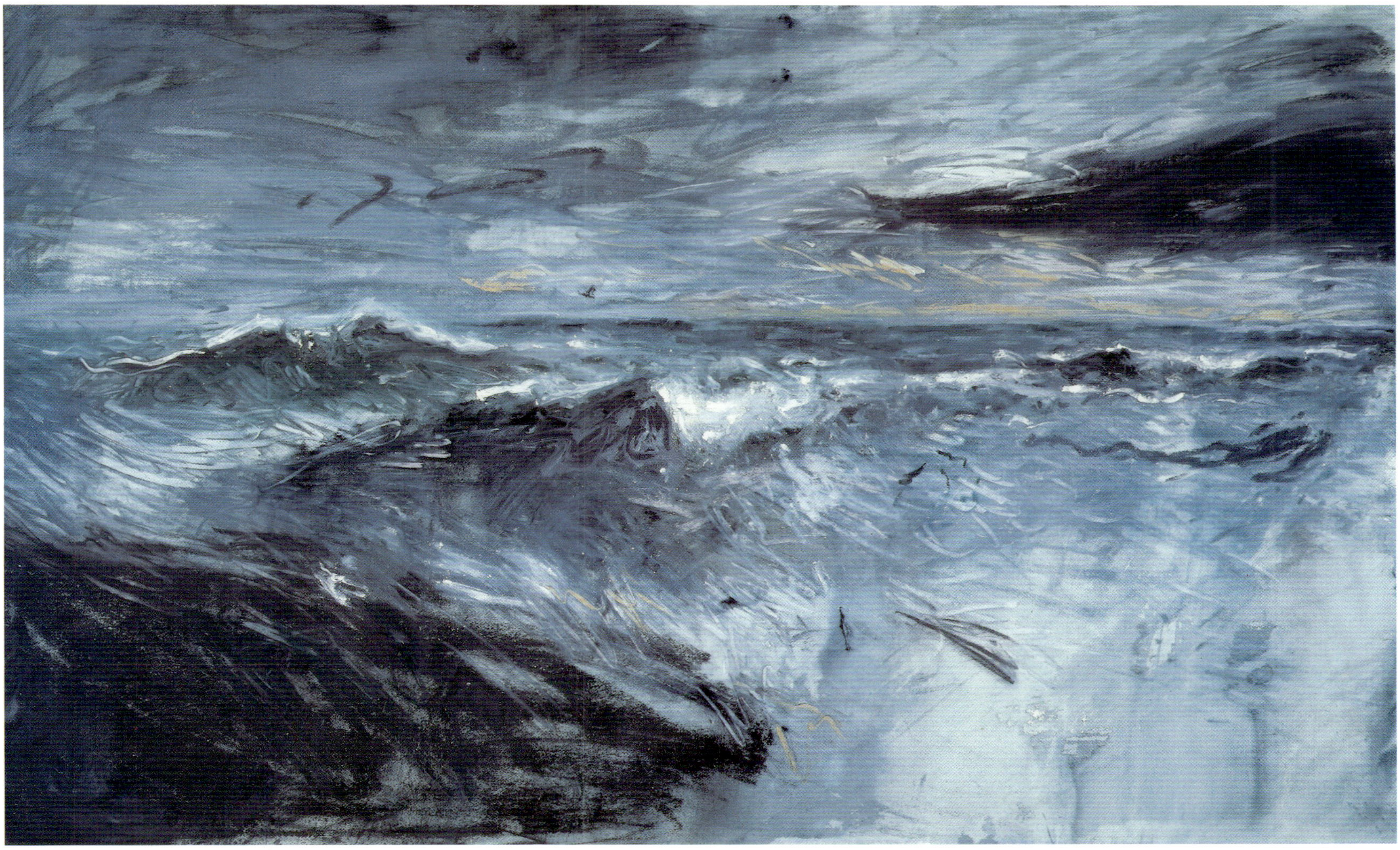

Waves breaking, late evening Bàgh nan Clach, Barra 1986. Watercolour & Conté 32″×54″.

Four studies from a book of paintings Barra 1986. 6¼″×22½″.

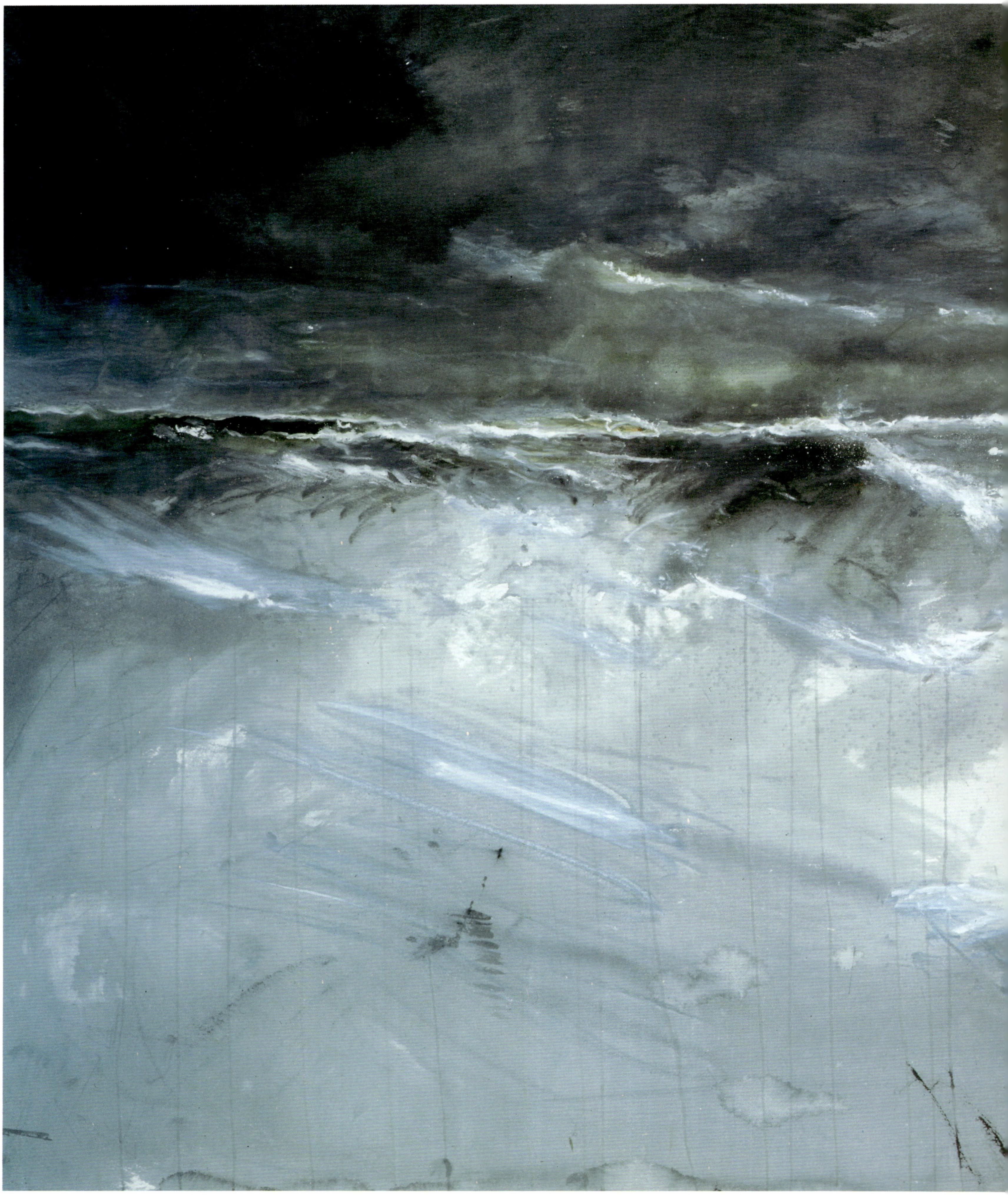

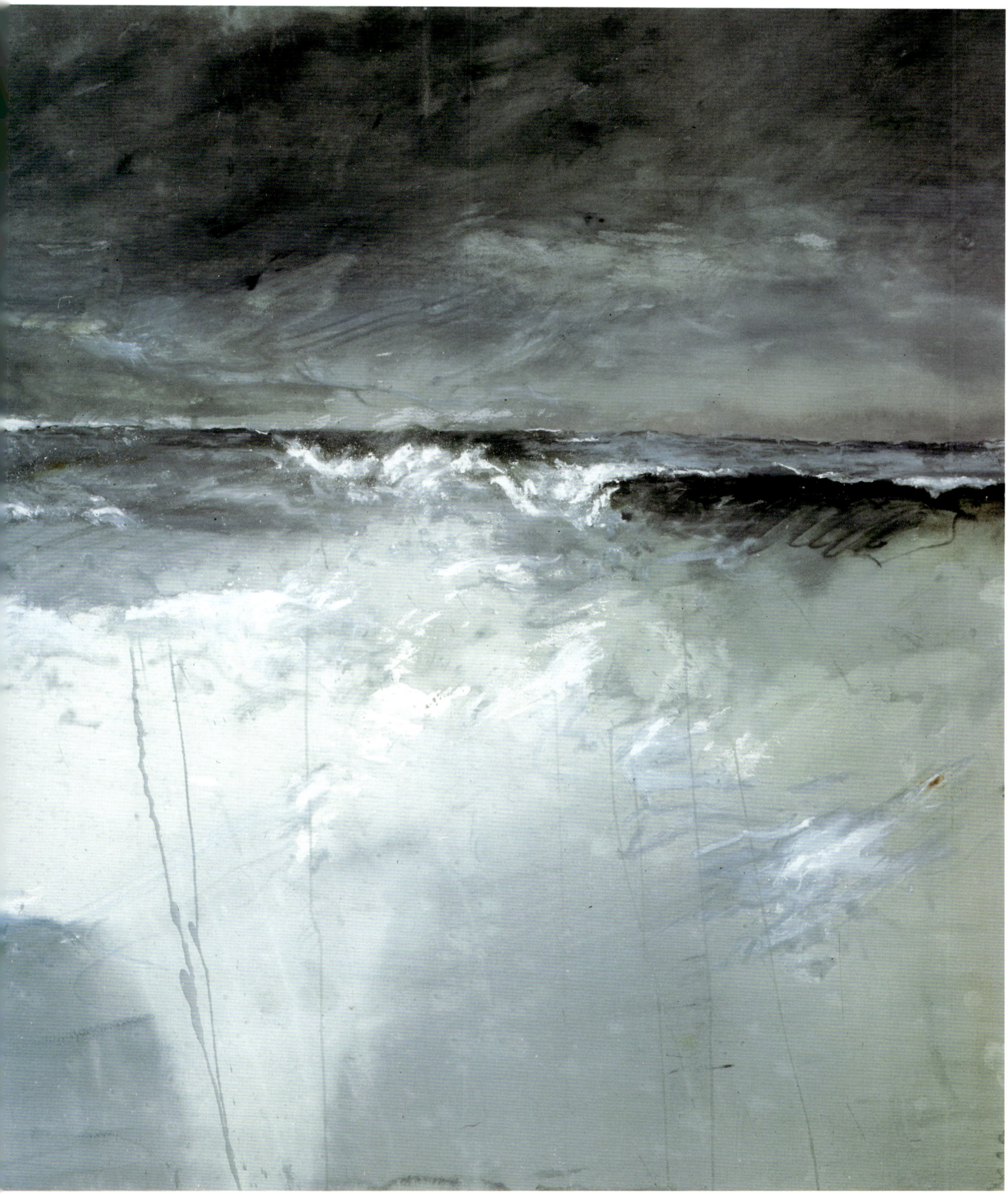

Sea Barra, very late evening 1986. Watercolour. 31″×53″.

Wave turning Barra 1986. Late evening. Watercolour. 31″×53″.

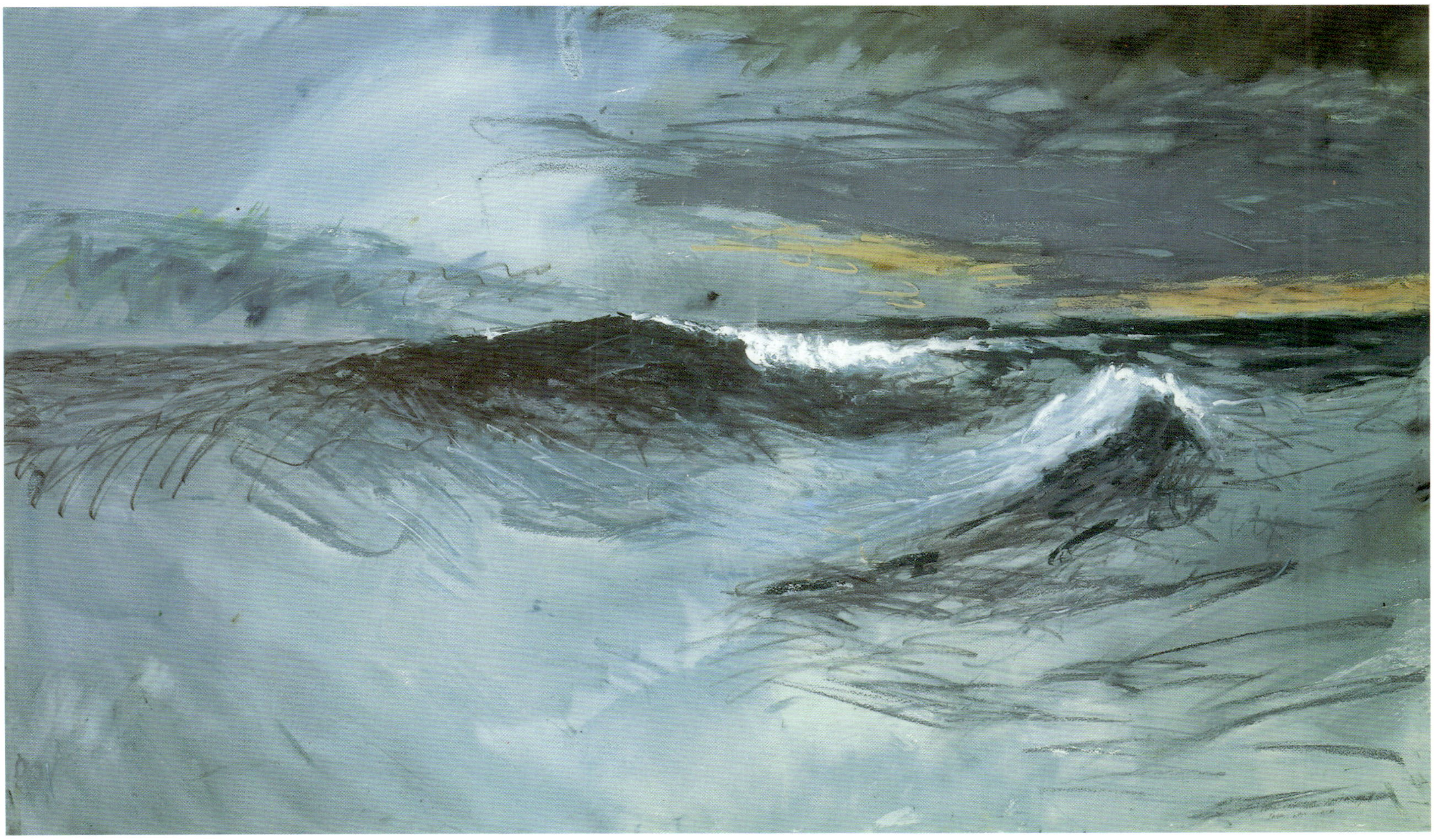

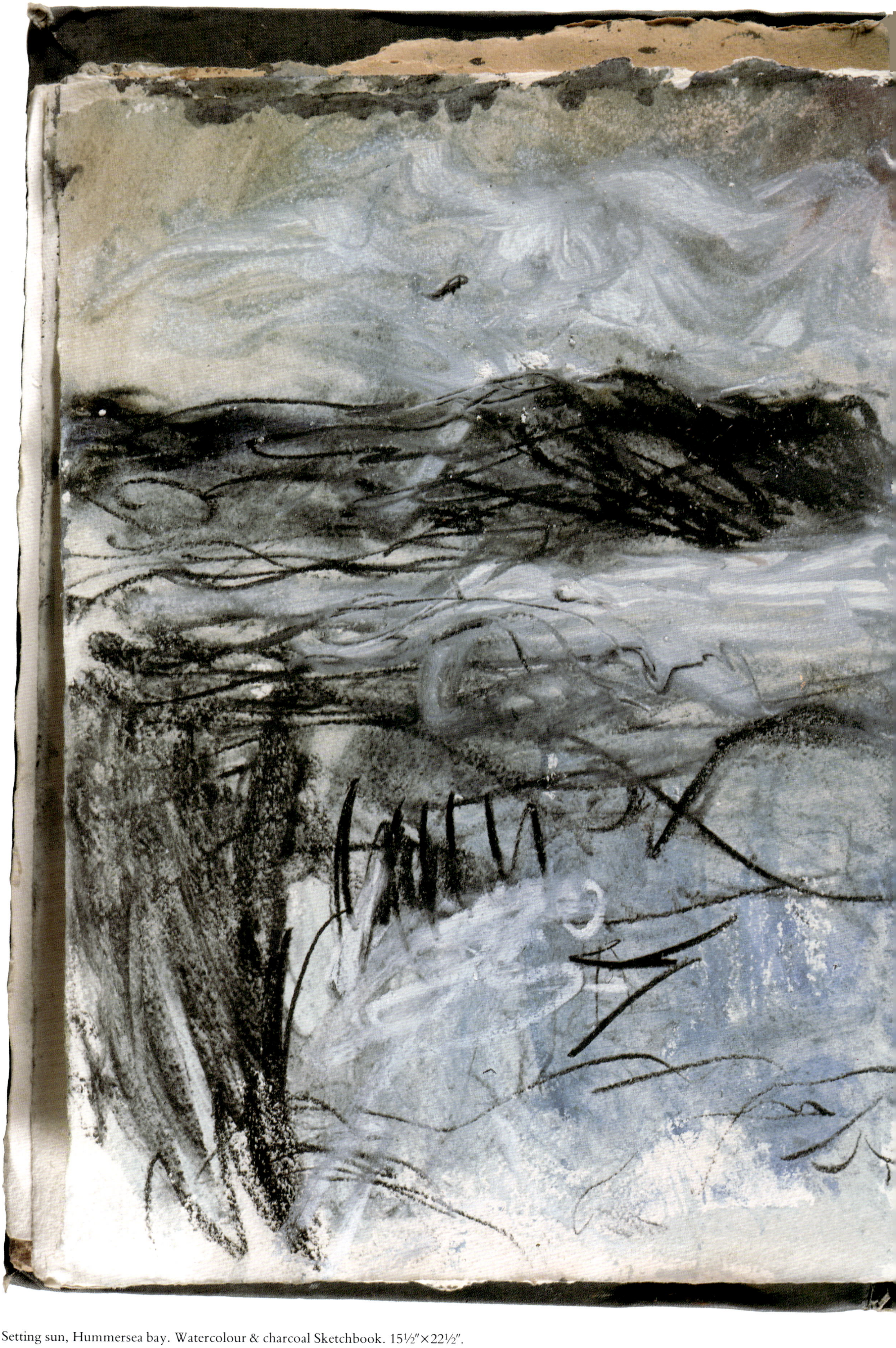

Setting sun, Hummersea bay. Watercolour & charcoal Sketchbook. 15½″×22½″.

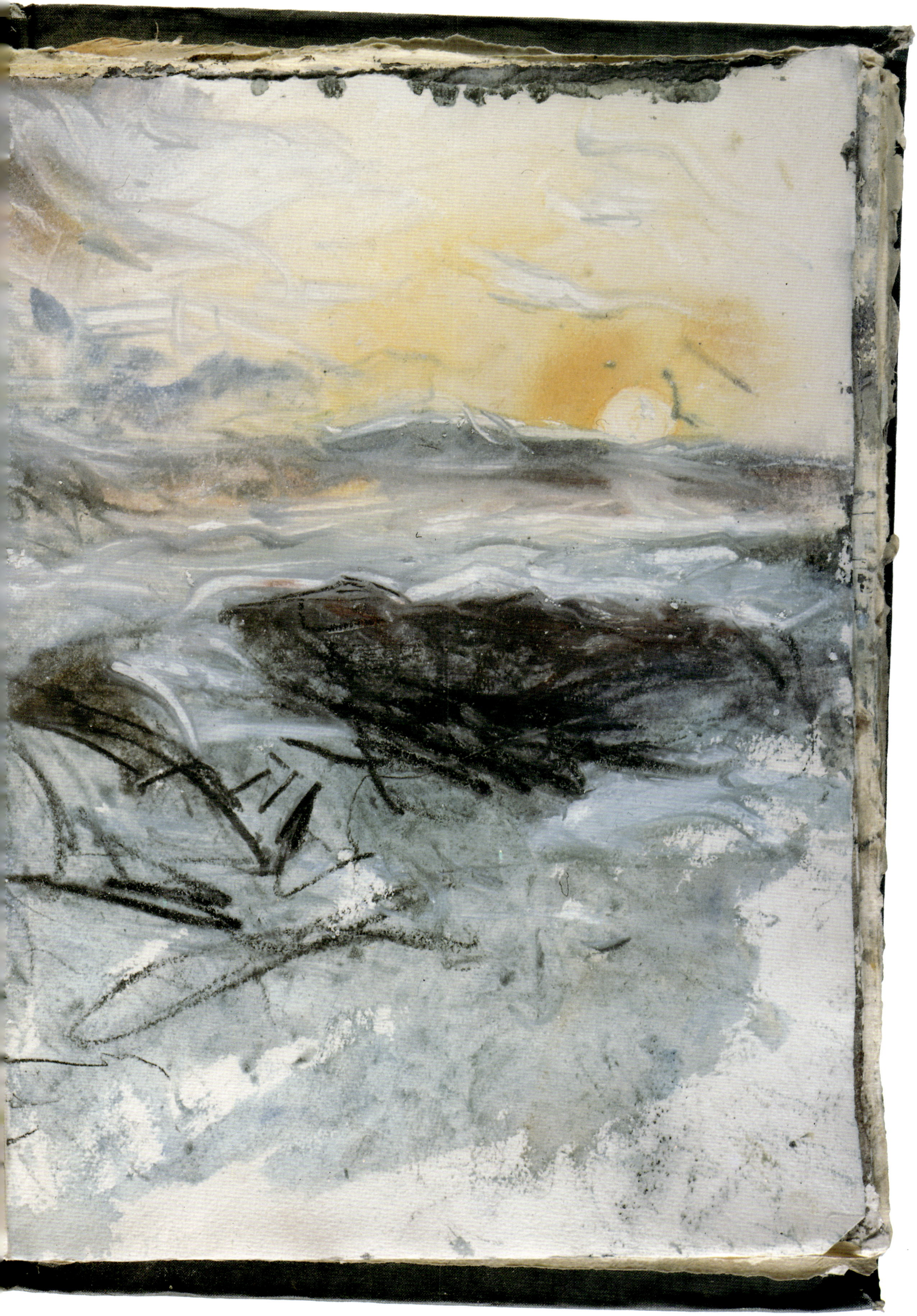

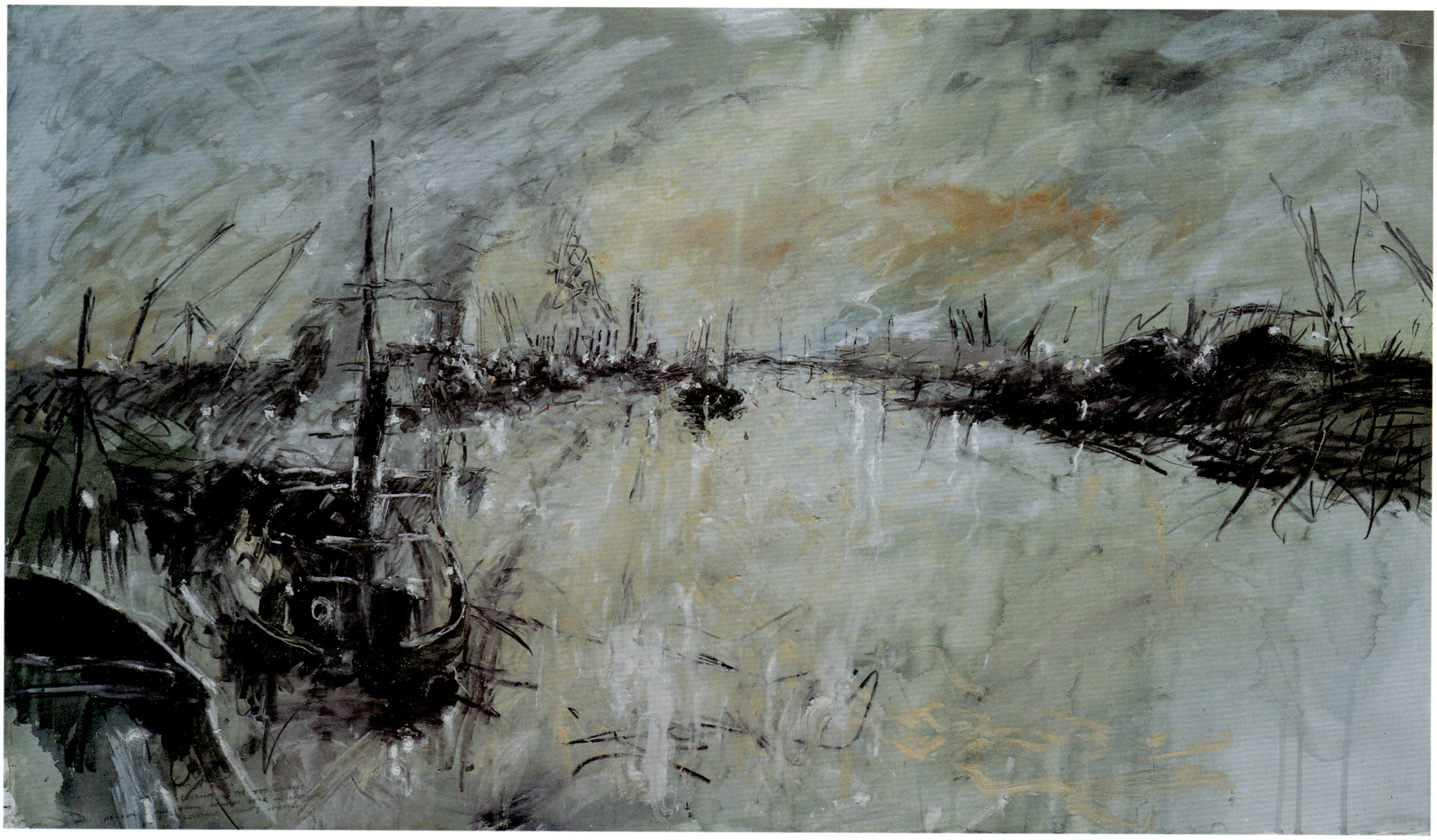

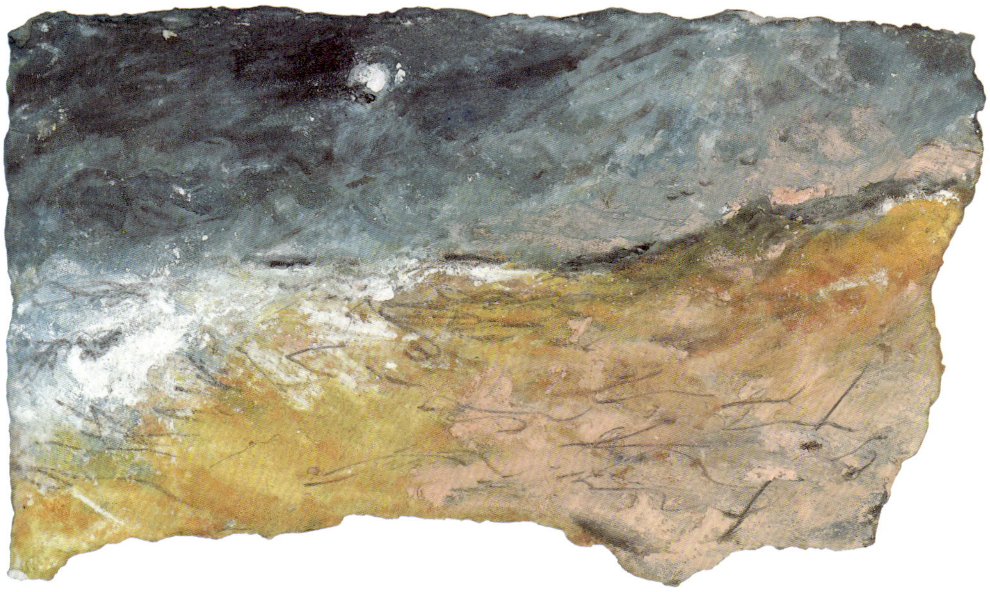

Looking up the Tees towards Haverton Hill and Bamlett's Bight, from the compass deck of the suction dredger 'Cleveland County' 10.00 p.m. Grab dredger 'Seal Sands' moored ahead. Watercolour & Conté. 31″×53″. Private Collection.

Lower. Coatham sands, full moon over Redcar, I. Watercolour on fragment of hand made paper, actual size.

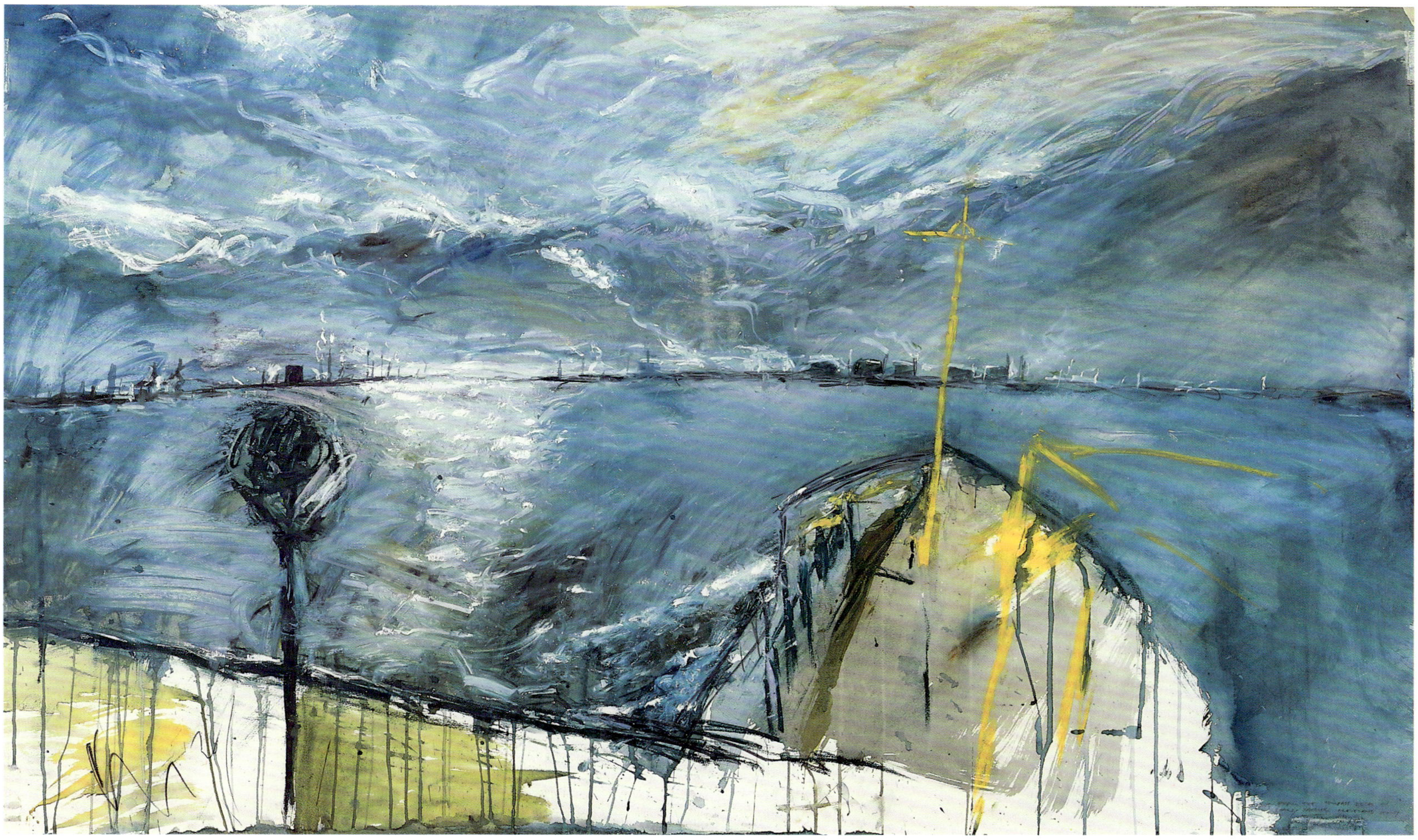

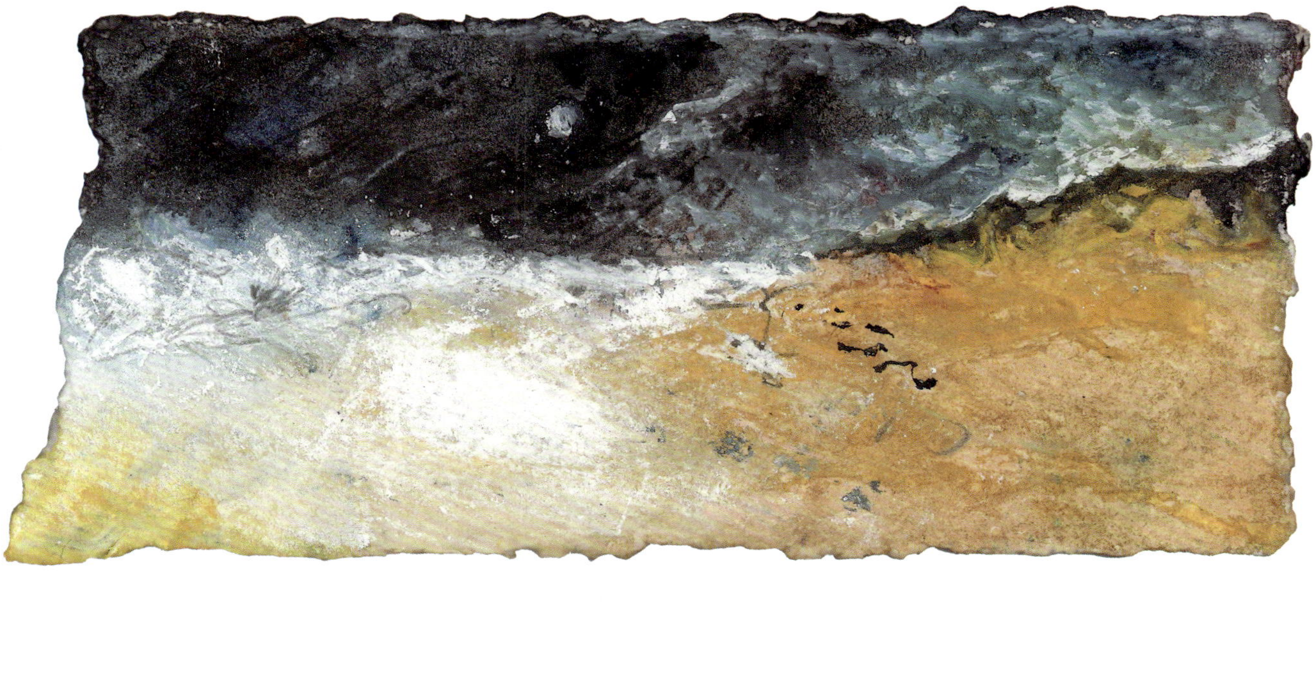

Stem of the suction dredger 'Cleveland County' turning back into the river Tees. Watercolour. 31″×53″.

Lower. Coatham sands, moon over Redcar, II. Watercolour on fragment of hand made paper, actual size.

Trinity House Light Vessel No. 8., in No. 4 dry dock at Smith's Shiprepairers, North Shields, being repainted after a re-fit.
1.00 a.m. September 1986. 40″×60″. Private collection.

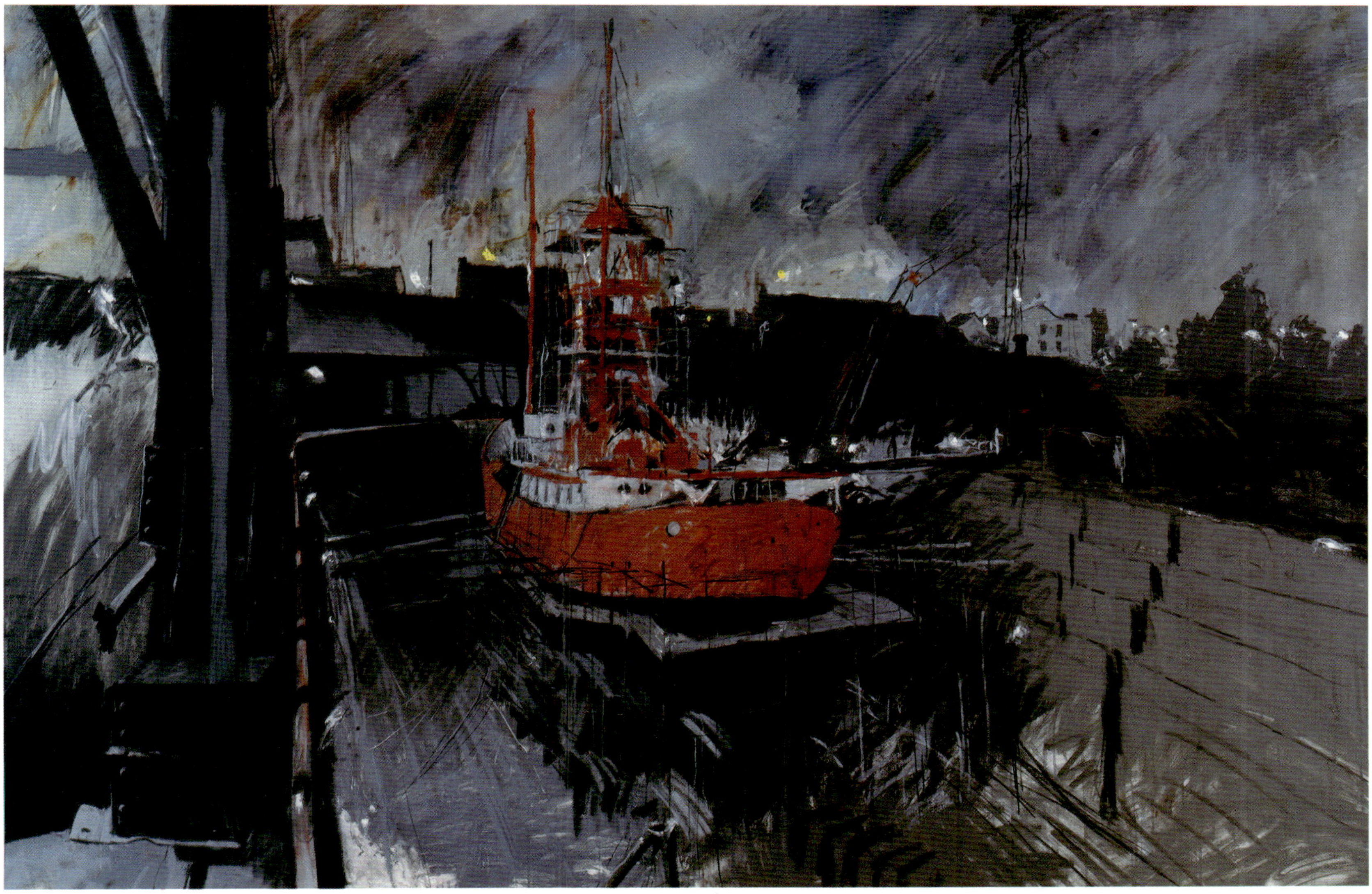

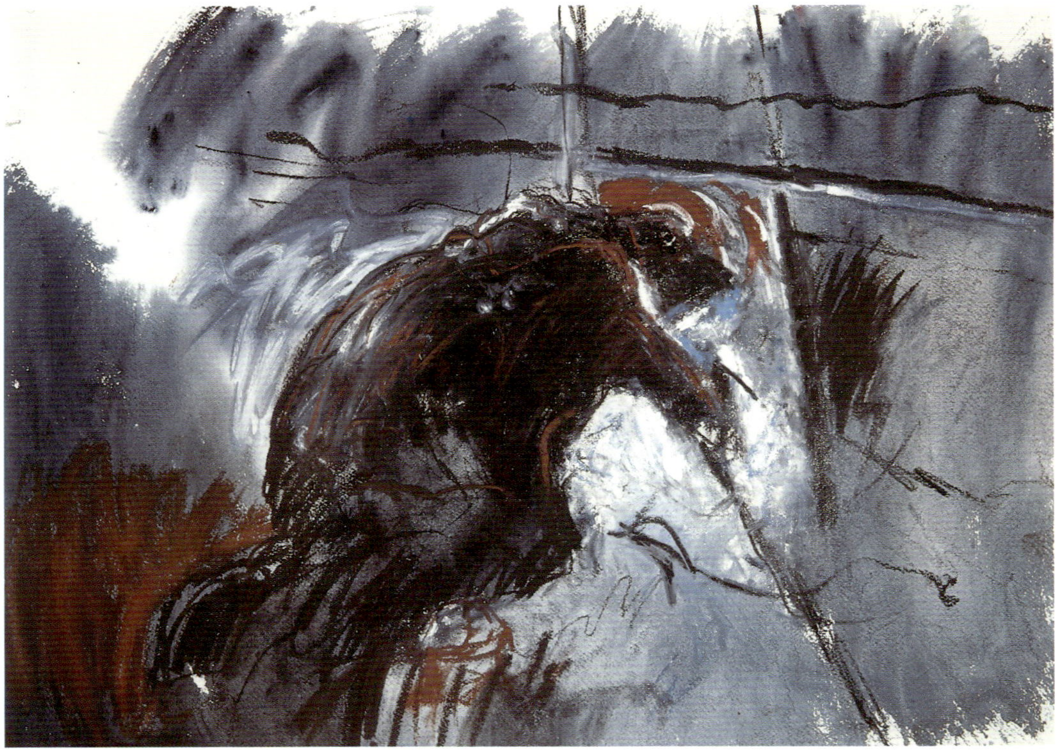

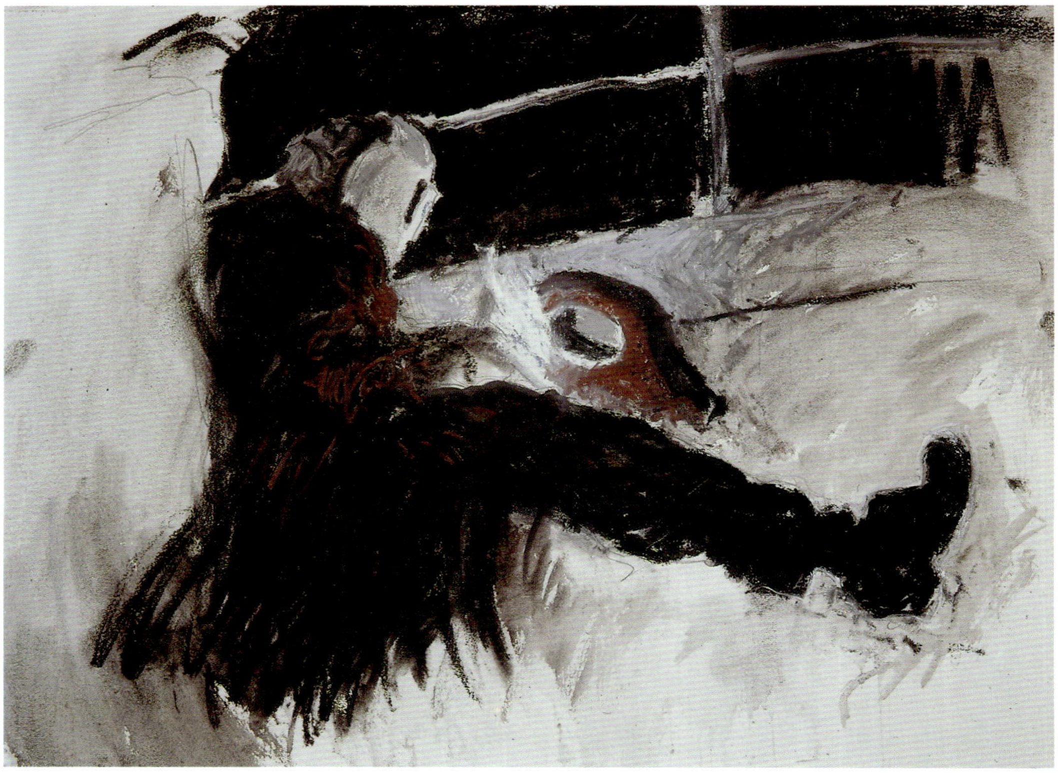

Two studies of Col' Marshall welding eye fittings onto the deck of 'North Islands' 3.00 a.m. December morning 1986. Hard frost on the deck, Smith's Dock Shipyard. Watercolour & pastel. 22″×30″. Private collection.

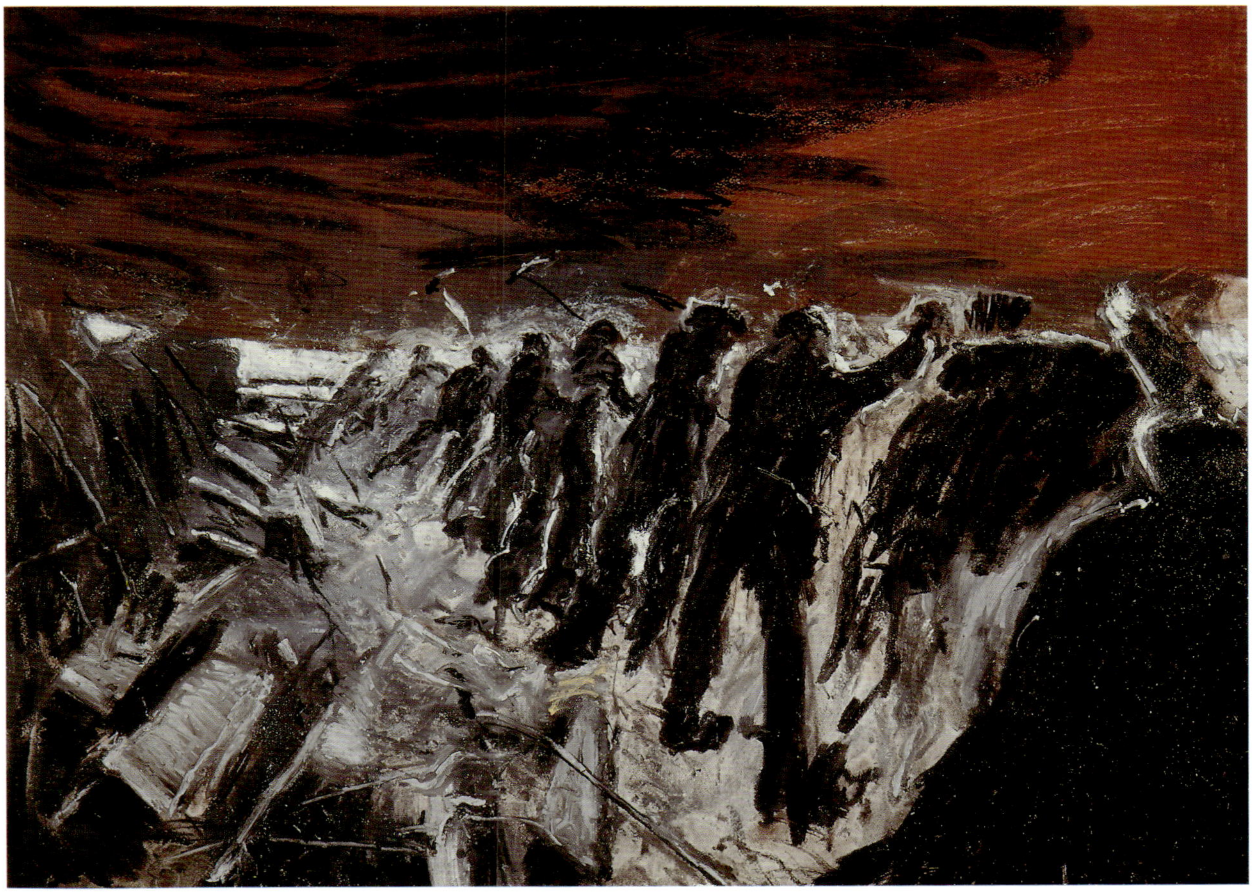

1.35 p.m. October 15th 1986. Shipwrights pushing out sand boxes underneath North Islands immediately before launch. The last ship to be built on the Tees. Watercolour. 22″×30″. Private collection.

Drilling. Roughnecks working in the drill house on the jack-up rig 'Britannia'. Southern North Sea. January 1988.
Watercolour. 22″×30″ (Detail) Conoco (U.K.) Ltd.

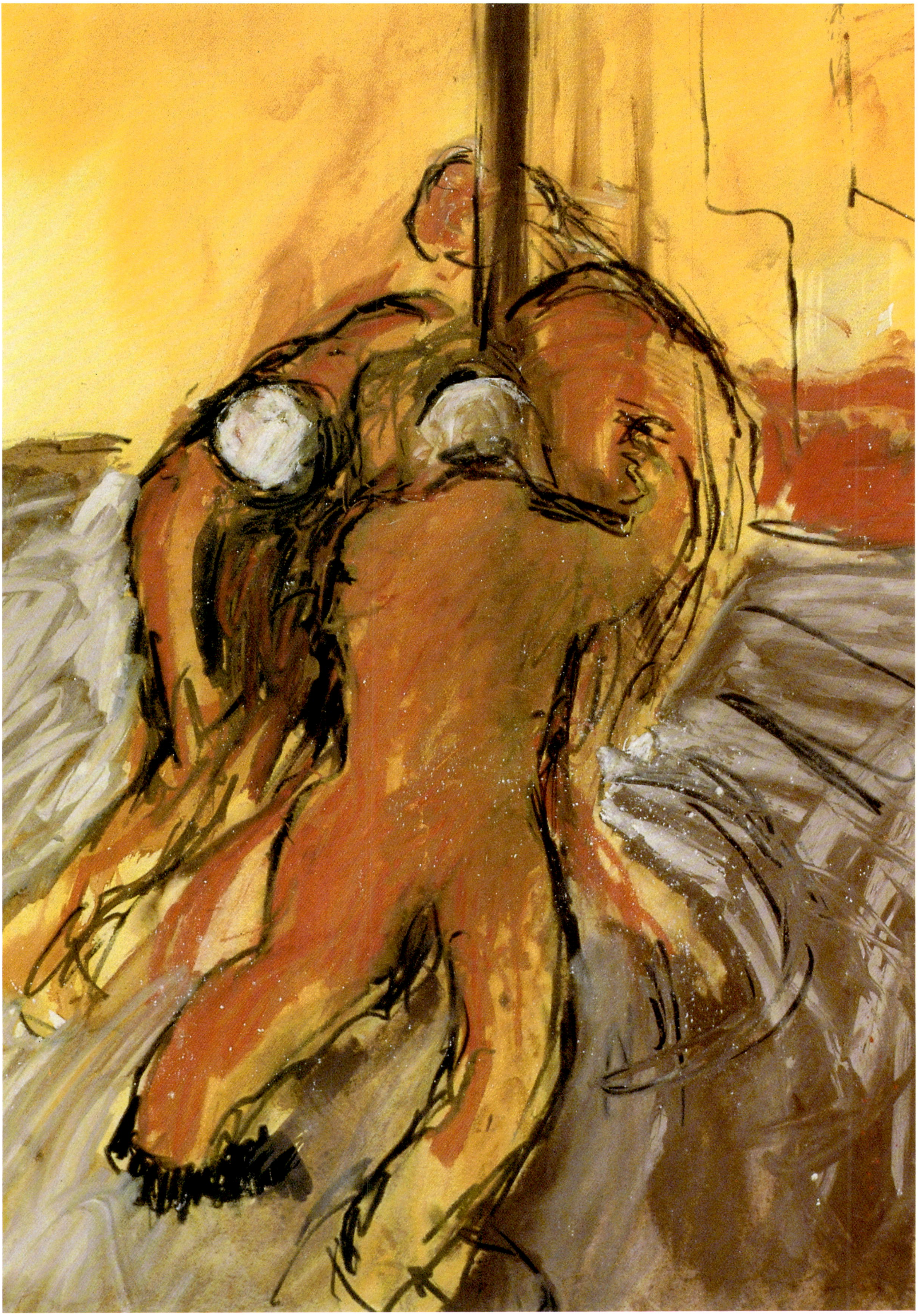

D.B. 102. from the starboard side of 'President Hubert' 26 Maart 1988. Heavy seas all day, gulls astern scavenging Michel's galley waste. Tow wire lying to starboard. Watercolour. 31″×53″.

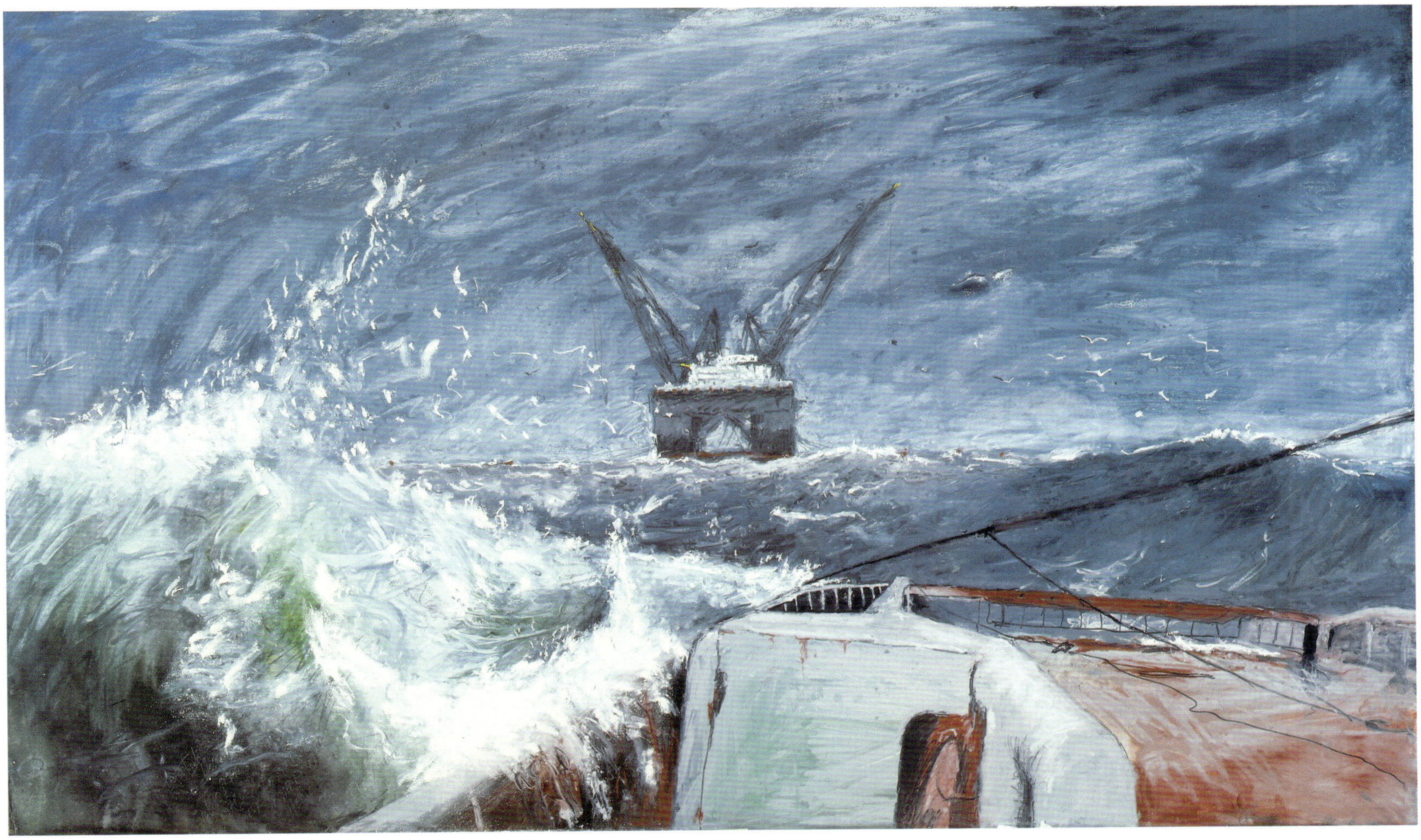

D.B.102. lifting accommodation module onto jacket, foggy morning North Valiant. March 1988. Southern North Sea.
Watercolour. 40″×60″. Conoco (UK) Ltd.

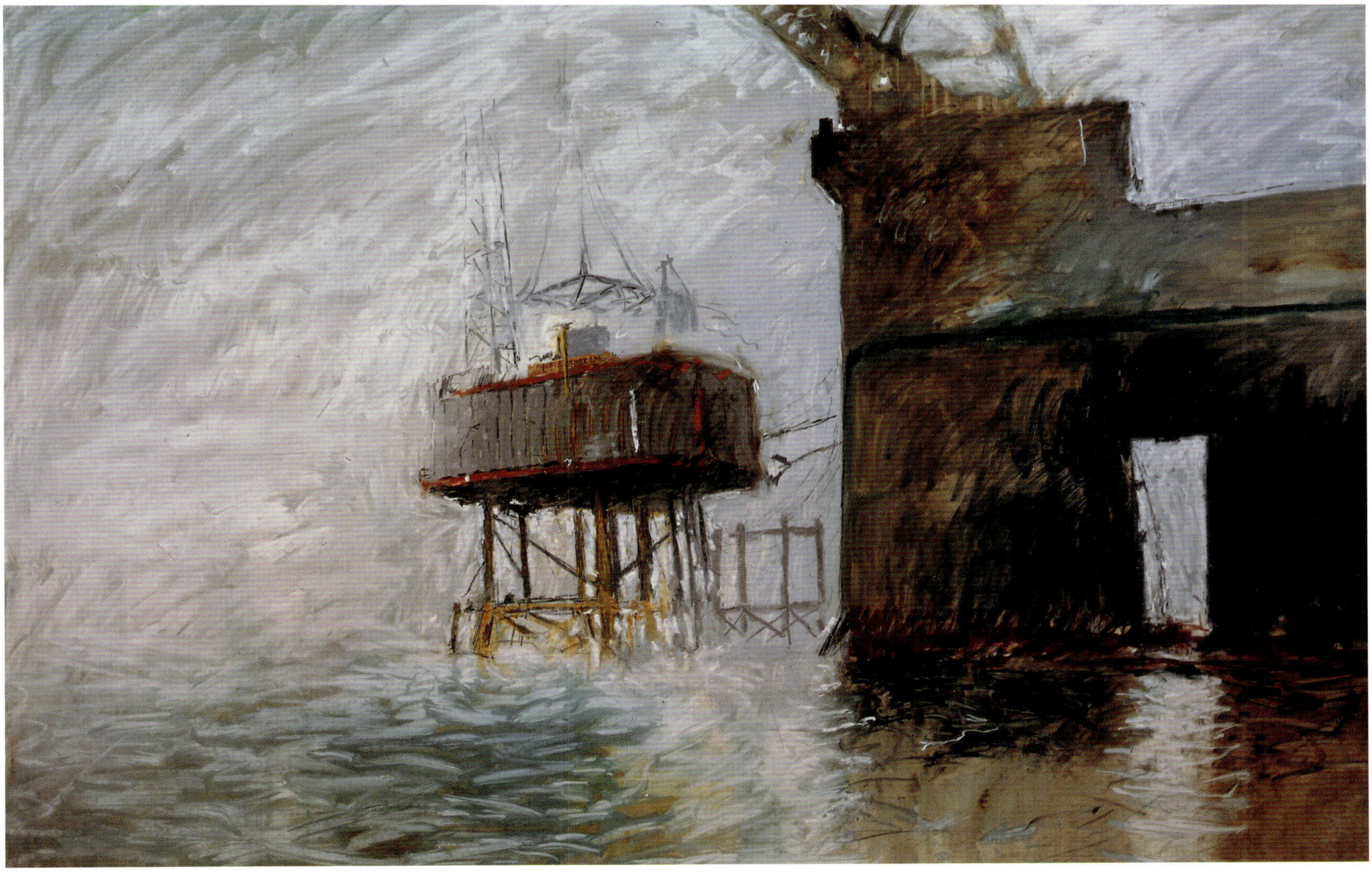

56° 99′ 81″ North, 002° 05′ East. Late afternoon Sunday 8th November 1987 raining steadily, sea rising. On board 'Oil Challenger,' chasing out anchors for semi-submersible rig 'Sea Explorer'. One 25 ton anchor lying on the deck, starboard side. 'Barra Supplier standing by with working lights showing, stand by vessel close in. Watercolour. 31″×53″.

Lower. Showery, early evening, Wednesday 11th November 1987 'Barra Supplier' lying alongside 'Sea Explorer,' now ballasted down. Ninian North beyond. Watercolour & pencil sketchbook. 11½″×15½″.

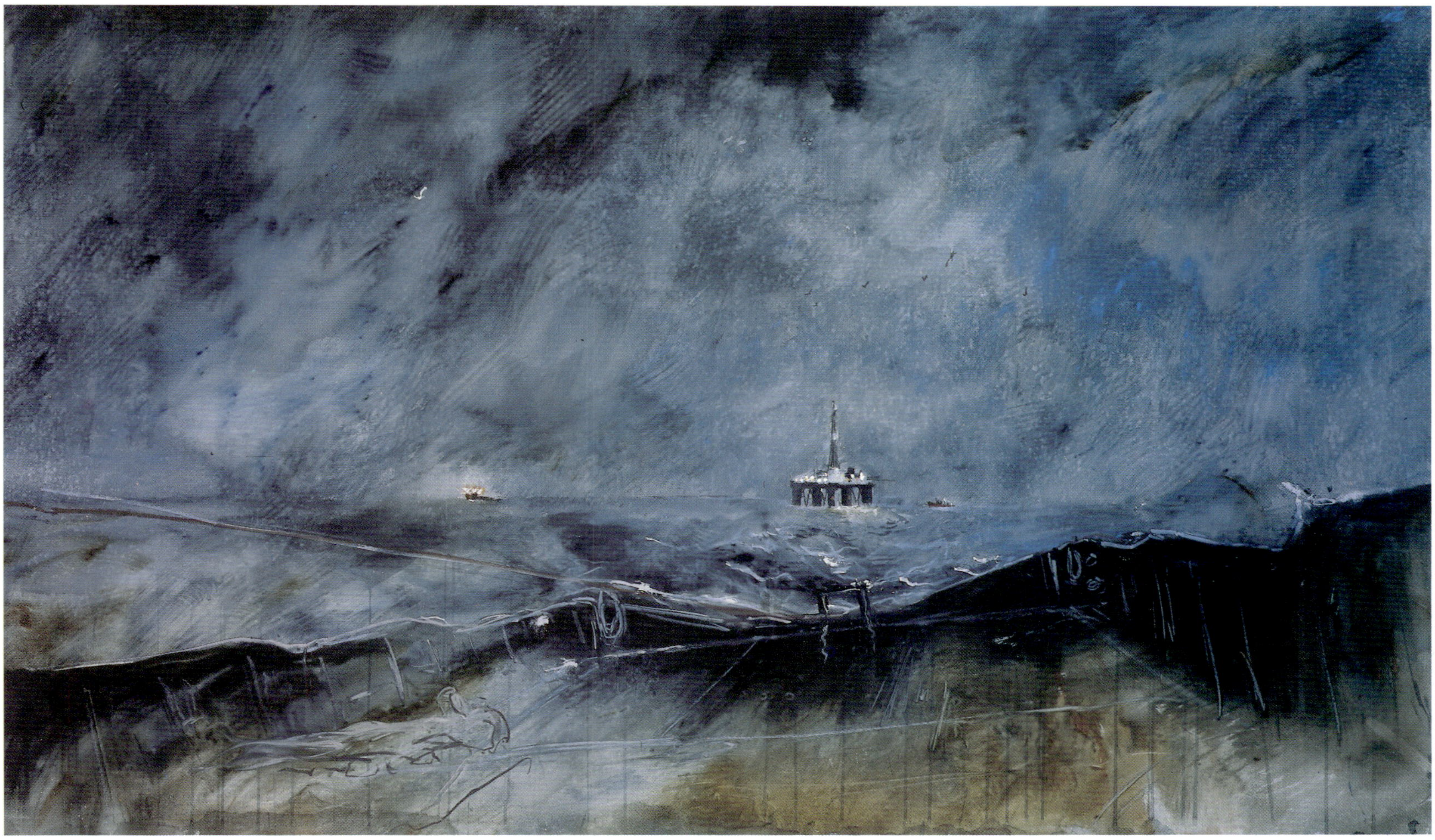

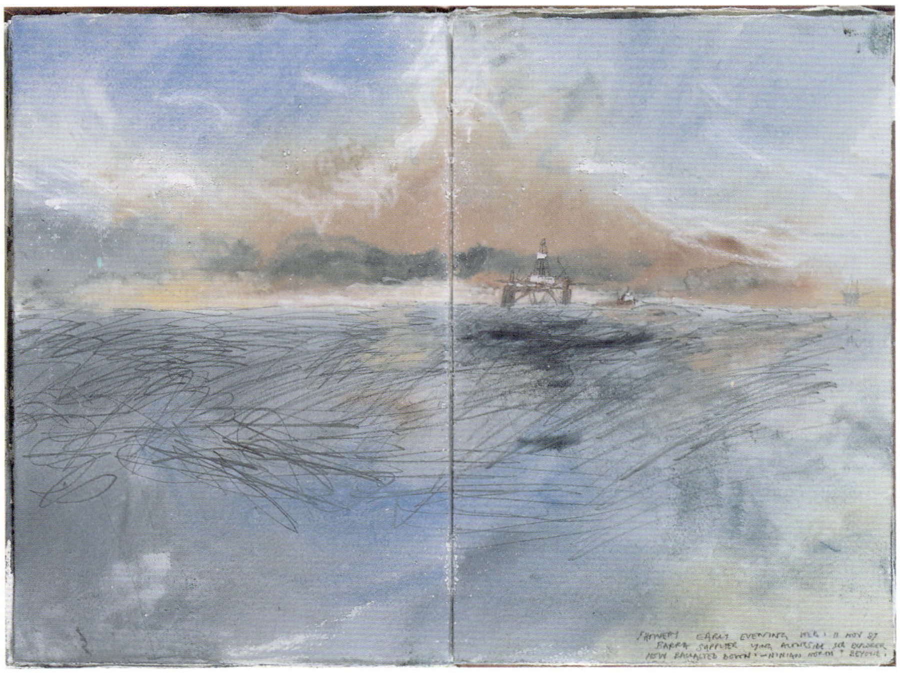
SHOWERY EARLY EVENING 11 NOV 87
BARRA SUPPLIER LYING ALONGSIDE SEA EXPLORER
NOW BALLASTED DOWN — NINIAN NORTH BEYOND

'Sea Explorer under tow, from Cod field, worked from the deck of 'Oil Challenger' Thundery afternoon. November 1987. Watercolour. 31″×53″.

Lower. Working anchors for 'Sea Explorer' 60° 45′ North 001° 34½′ East. 'Alwyn'? on skyline, fresh south easterly. Sketchbook 11″×31″.

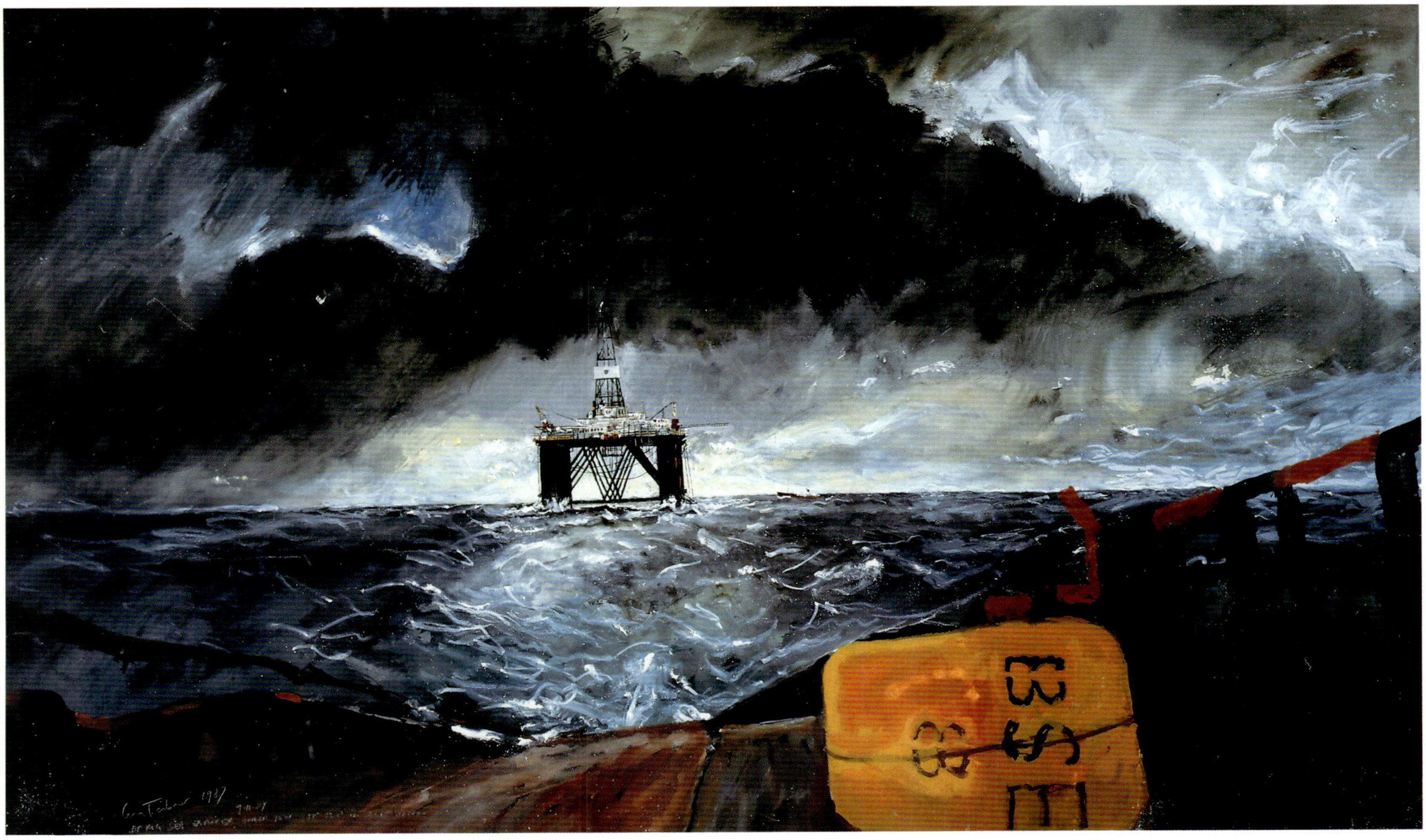

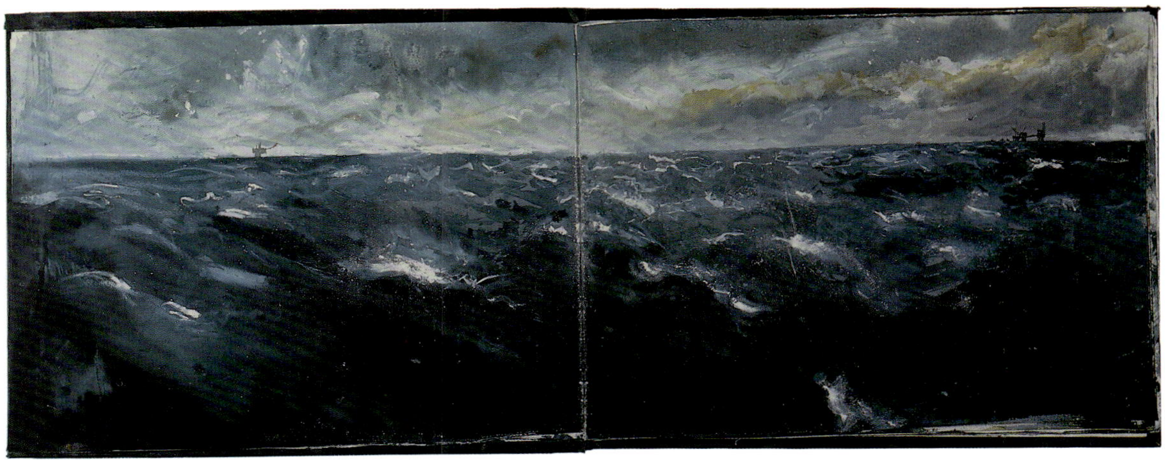

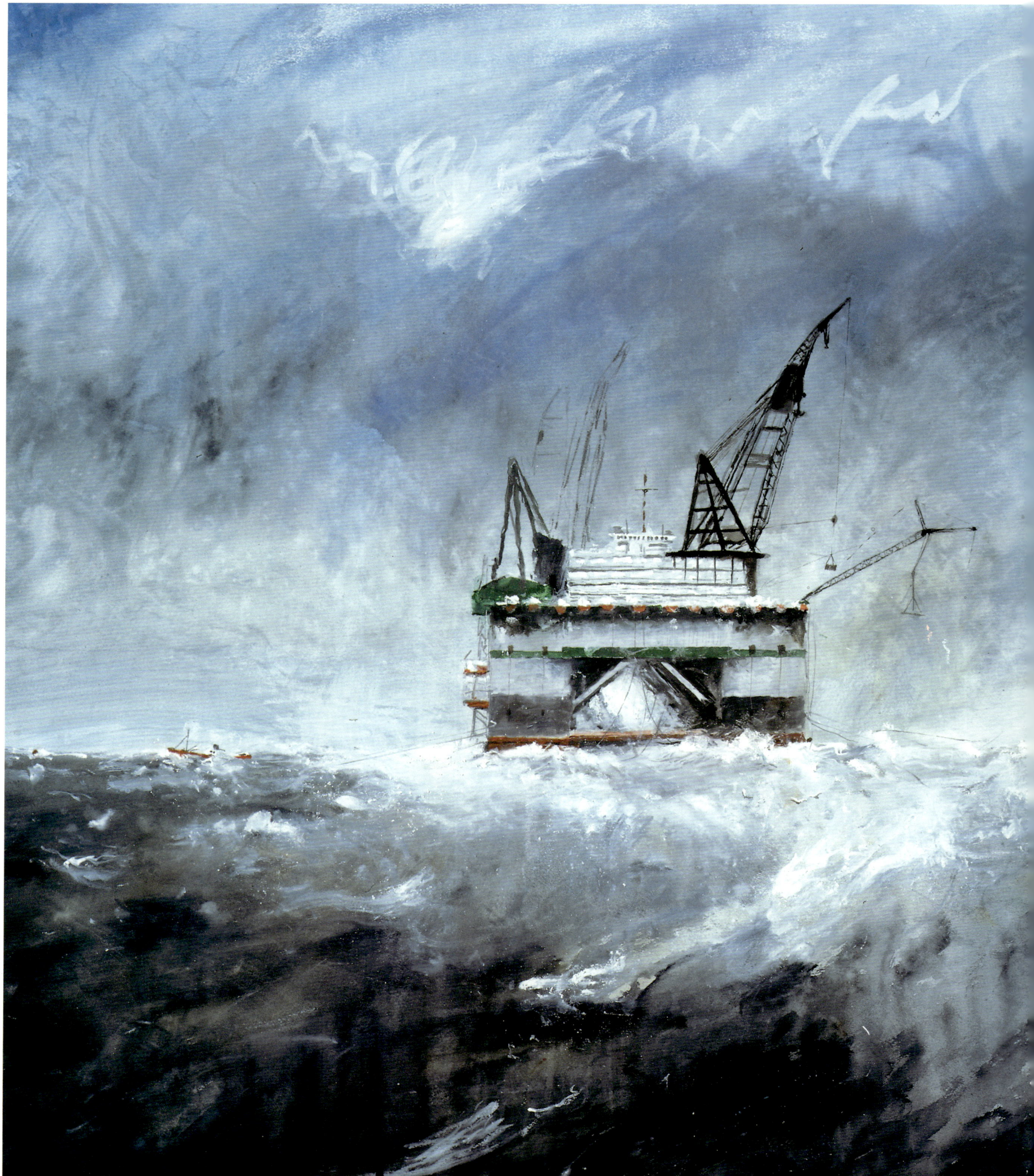

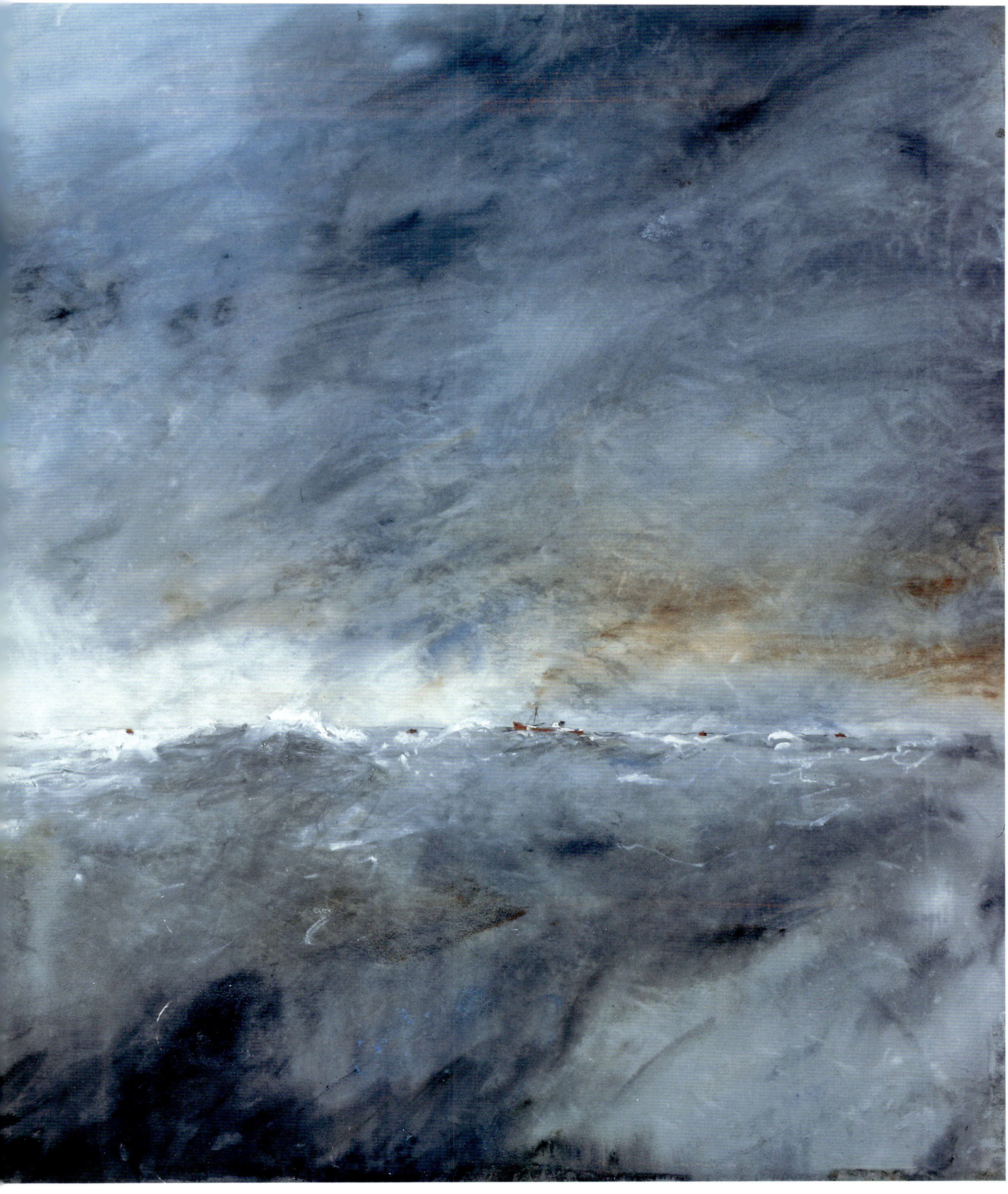

D.B.102. from 'President Hubert' March 1988. Watercolour. 31″×53″.

Gusty day, stiff gale blowing, southern North Sea. Jack up rigs, 'Moray Firth' and 'Penhrod 92' drilling North Valiant I and II for Conoco, standing on the cantilever deck on 'Britannia' January 1988. Watercolour. 31″×53″.

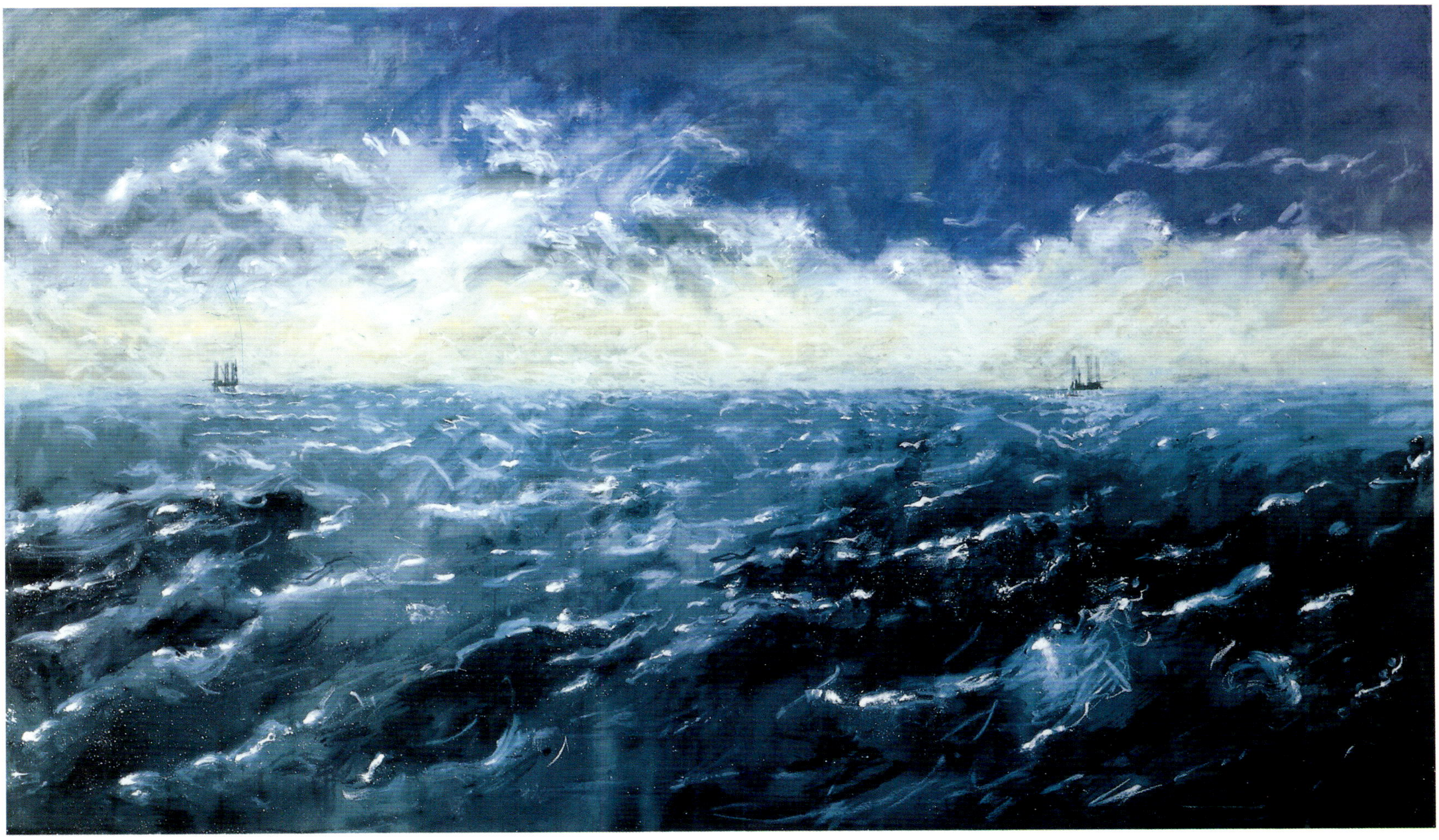

Cod field, backing up to 'Sea Explorer' 1 a.m., chasing out anchors and preparing to tow. 'Barra Supplier' standing by. From the deck of 'Oil Challenger' November 1987. Watercolour. 26½″×41″.

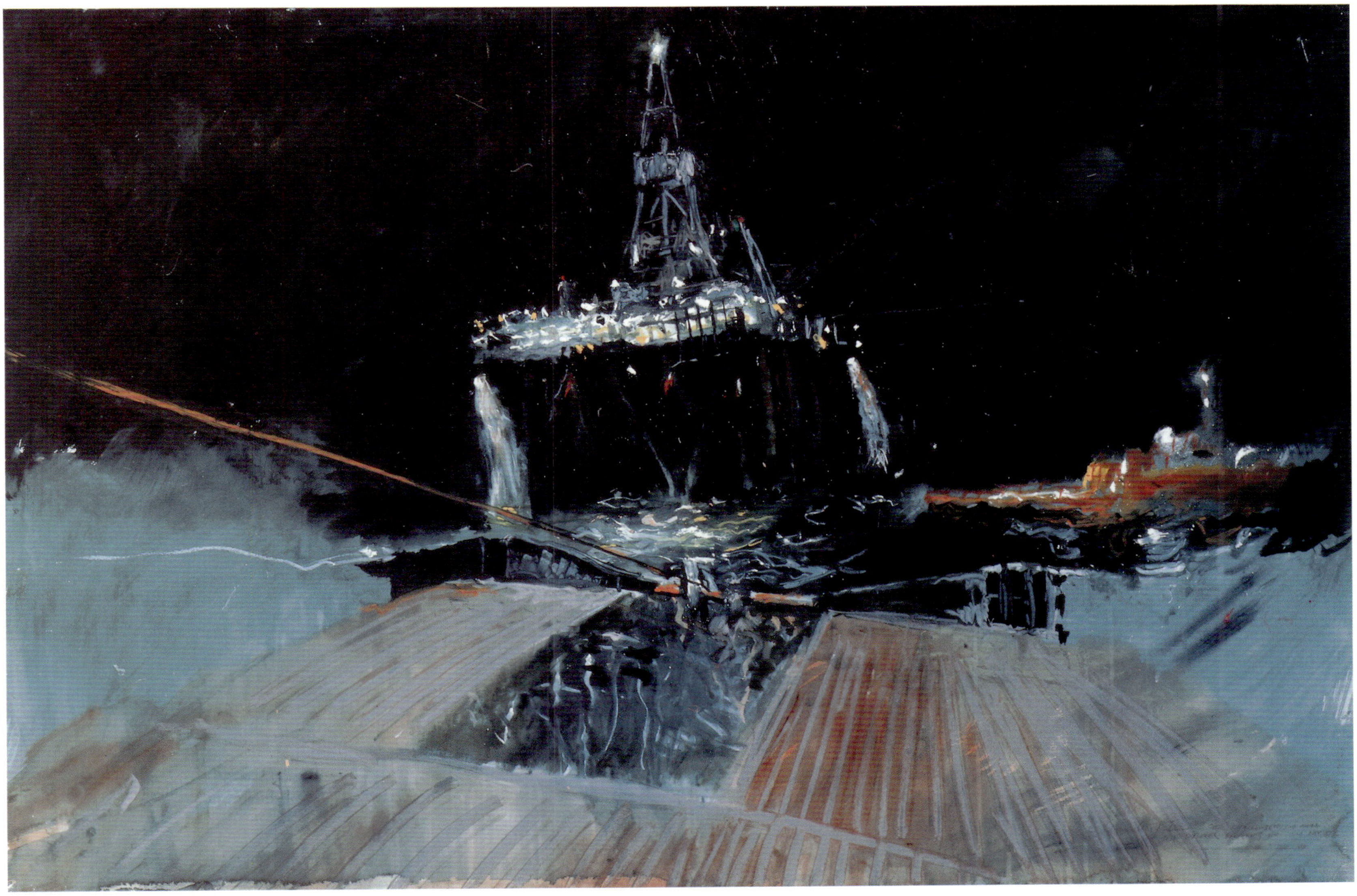

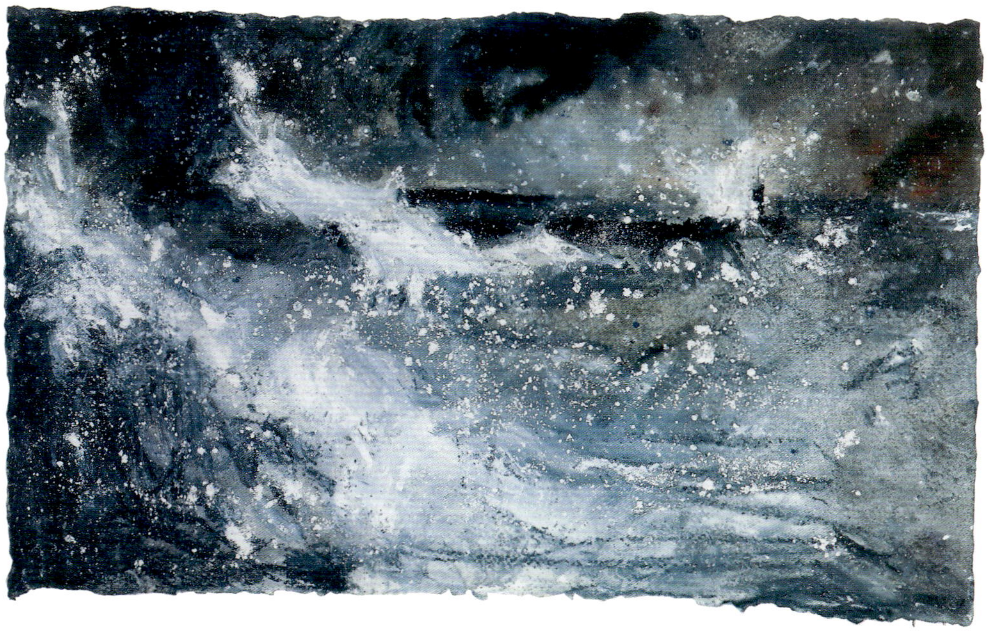

My work is concerned with the experience of being in, rather than merely looking at, the landscape. I am trying to express the whole feeling of being present in a place as well as the presence of the place itself. The work is necessarily concerned with space and the expression of the feeling, not only of space but of those elements which fill the space. Air – dry or wet, cold or warm – still or storm blown. I am concerned as much with the tactile aspects of the landscape as those that are visual.

In many of the landscapes I am trying to draw the wind and the weather as much as the forms of the land itself.

I hope that some of the work will eventually have a small amount of the vitality and strength that I see and feel in the things around me and that through the work, these things will be shared.

Len Tabner.

Heavy seas breaking. Staithes harbour-mouth early evening. Watercolour & Conte.